中文联盟
ChinesePlus

U0828787

HSK
标准会话教程 2
HSK Standard Conversational Course 2

HSK BIAOZHUN HUIHUA JIAOCHENG 2

中文联盟平台教学中心 语文出版社教材研究中心 编写
Co-edited by Chinese Plus Platform Teaching and Learning Center and Textbook Research Center of Language & Culture Press

张 会 主编
Lead Author Zhang Hui

语文出版社
·北京·

汉考国际认证
适用于汉语水平考试（HSK）

总策划：谷新矿　静　炜
策　划：邵亦鹏　李佩泽　郑　浩　朱春玲

项目负责人：王锦红
项目组成员：许雪松　姜天琦　孙博雅
黄　蕾　王　轩　高　鹤　李艳娇

主　　编：张　会
英文翻译：Raluca Georgescu（张　露）

图书在版编目（CIP）数据

HSK标准会话教程. 2 / 中文联盟平台教学中心，语文出版社教材研究中心编写 ; 张会主编. -- 北京 : 语文出版社，2021.10(2025.6重印)
ISBN 978-7-5187-1353-0

Ⅰ. ①H… Ⅱ. ①中… ②语… ③张… Ⅲ. ①汉语－口语－对外汉语教学－水平考试－教材 Ⅳ. ①H195.4

中国版本图书馆CIP数据核字(2021)第147607号

责任编辑　许雪松
装帧设计　徐晓森
出　　版　语文出版社
地　　址　北京市东城区朝阳门内南小街51号　100010
电子信箱　ywcbsywp@163.com
排　　版　北京光大印艺文化发展有限公司
印刷装订　北京市科星印刷有限责任公司
发　　行　语文出版社　新华书店经销
规　　格　890mm×1240mm
开　　本　1/16
印　　张　7.75
字　　数　134千字
版　　次　2021年10月第1版
印　　次　2025年6月第3次印刷
定　　价　76.00元

010-65592964(咨询)　010-65240052(购书)　010-65250075(印装质量)

前言

本系列教材《HSK标准会话教程》共5册，根据汉语水平考试（HSK）大纲一级至四级和汉语水平口语考试（HSKK）大纲初级和中级设计，1—3册分别对应HSK一级、二级、三级大纲，4—5册对应HSK四级大纲。各册教材以《普通话1000句》为蓝本，合理吸收其话题与典型句式，以“考教结合”为目标，“以考促教”“以考促学”，学习者学完每一册后可以获得相应的口语交际能力，参加相应级别汉语水平考试。

在编写理念上，本系列教材吸收了国际中文教学研究成果，遵循教学规律，强调典型语境的示范作用，培养学习者对所学词语的多场景重新组合能力。同时，结合时代发展和教学法革新的需求，借鉴移动学习、在线学习的教学理念，研发了配套动漫和微课，使静态的图书与动态的视频有机结合起来，让学习的过程更加有趣，途径更加宽广，手段更加多样，学习的效果更加显著。教师可以拥有丰富的教学内容和灵活的教学手段，学习者可以拥有活泼的学习气氛和多样的学习形式。

本系列教材的特色：

第一，用框架突出句子结构。在“热身”部分采用独特的图形框架展示句子的结构特点及句型的变换关系，让句子结构一目了然，对培养学习者语言输出过程中的组句能力和语言听读过程中的断句能力非常有帮助。

第二，文化理解促进语言学习。每一课的文化点都是与课文内容相关的文化常识或现当代中国国情，有助于学习者了解语言中蕴含的文化因素和中国的现状，加深对中国语言文化的深层次理解，进而促进语言的学习。

第三，对话与陈述并重。每一课在对话体课文外都提供一个第三人称角度的陈述性段落，不同级别对段落的长短、词语的难度要求不同，目的是从入门阶段就开始培养学习者的语段表达能力，即使是在一级阶段词汇数量不多的情况下，也要让所学的每一个词都能得到充分的运用。

第四，侧重听说技能。课文方面，在词汇大纲范围内，尽量通过日常生活常见的情景，展现中文对话中常用的词语和句子。练习题模拟汉语水平考试题型，围绕听说技能的发展进行训练，具有很强的实用性。

第五，配套资源丰富多样。对话及课后听力练习全部配有音频，方便学习者预习、跟读及教师教学，注重培养学习者在不同情景中得体恰当地运用中文进行交际的能力。第一册和第二册配套“动画课文”，将静态、无声的课文变成有声有色的动画故事，增强了教材的趣味性、可读性，帮助学习者理解对话的含义。第三册至第五册配套短视频微课，为教师教授语法和重点词语或进行翻转课堂教学提供条件，也利于学习者课下预习或复习。具体内容可参阅“中文联盟平台”专题网页（http://hskc.chineseplus.net）。

本系列教材在研发过程中得到了语文出版社、五洲网络和汉考国际的大力支持和指导，收到了来自五大洲上百所孔子学院（课堂）中外方院长、教师及中国高校中文教师的意见反馈，集中了众多关心中文教材编纂人士的智慧。我们谨代表编写组对大家表示最衷心的感谢。尽管我们竭尽所能，但仍不免存在这样那样的不足，恳请广大师生和读者朋友在使用过程中随时向我们反馈意见，以便将来进一步完善，使本系列教材能够成为广大中文学习者的好帮手。

编写组

2021 年 7 月

Preface

This ***HSK Standard Conversational Course*** series consists of five volumes, designed in accordance with *HSK Test Syllabus* (HSK Levels I-IV) and *Chinese Proficiency Test Syllabus Speaking* (HSKK Primary and Intermediate Levels). Volumes 1 to 3 correspond to the HSK Levels I to III syllabi, and volumes 4 and 5 correspond to the HSK Level IV syllabus. The content for each level is based on *1000 Mandarin Chinese Sentences*, from which various topics and marker sentences are assimilated in a way that fits the intended purposes, namely to "combine testing with teaching" "promote teaching through testing", and "promote learning through testing". Upon completion of each volume, learners will have the necessary communication skills and will be able to attend the corresponding HSK test.

The writing concepts behind this conversational Chinese textbook series draw on research results in the field of teaching Chinese as a foreign language, adhere to teaching rules, and lay stress on the illustrative role typical contexts play, in order to cultivate learners' ability to make full use of the words and expressions they've learned by adapting them to various new contexts. Moreover, changing trends of the times and the need for innovation in pedagogy are considered carefully, thus the following notions are applied: use teaching and learning concepts of mobile learning and online learning for reference, develop animations and micro-lectures to complement the textbooks, and integrate the static with the dynamic by using both textbooks and videos, all these with the purpose of having a more engaging learning process, more extensive channels, and more varied methods, which will ultimately lead to remarkable learning results. Teachers will benefit from the rich teaching content and the flexible teaching methods, while students will enjoy a lively learning atmosphere and varied forms of learning.

The five features of this series are:

First, use of boxes to emphasize sentence structures. In the "Warm-up" section, each sentence is enclosed in distinctive drawn boxes which indicate the sentence structure characteristics and show how sentences may convert from one individual word to a larger chunk, thus making sentence structures become clear at a glance. This system greatly helps cultivate learners' ability to form sentences during the process of language output as well as their ability to break down sentences during the process of listening and reading.

Second, comprehension of cultural aspects boosts the language learning process. The cultural aspects presented in each lesson are in close connection with the content of the texts, being either pieces of general cultural knowledge about China or knowledge specifically regarding modern and contemporary China. These will greatly help cultivate learners' understanding of the cultural elements hidden beneath the language layer and the present situation in China and give them a deeper insight into Chinese language and culture, thus acting as catalysts for the language learning process.

Third, equal importance is attached to both dialogues and narration. Each lesson contains a narrative paragraph presented in the third person to complement the active dialogues. The length of the paragraphs and the difficulty level of the words used differ depending on different levels. The purpose is to cultivate learners' discourse ability right from the threshold level and allow them to make full use of every word they've learned even when they're at Level I with a limited vocabulary.

Fourth, lay stress on speaking and listening skills. By staying within the limits of the HSK vocabulary, the texts employ numerous common scenarios from everyday life to display words and sentences frequently used in Chinese conversation. The drills simulate actual HSK question types, by focusing on training listening and speaking skills in a very practical way.

Fifth, a wide variety of auxiliary resources is offered all throughout the series. All the dialogues and listening drills come with audio recordings, which are very handy for both students to prepare the lessons before class or read along and for teachers to conduct their lessons. These lay emphasis on cultivating learners' ability to communicate in Chinese appropriately and effectively in various contexts. Volume 1 and 2 come with "anime texts", which transform the static, soundless texts into stories full of sound and color, making the books more engaging and more readable, thus helping learners grasp the meaning of the dialogues. Volume 3 to 5 come with short videos of micro-lectures, which are a good resource for teachers to present grammar and key words and expressions or to adopt a flipped classroom system for teaching, as well as for learners to prepare or review lessons. For more details, see the special page under Chinese Plus Platform: http://hskc.chineseplus.net.

During its research and development, this series has received strong support and guidance from Language & Culture Press, Continental Network and Chinese Testing International (CTI). Moreover, generous feedback was presented by Chinese and local directors and teachers from more than one hundred Confucius Institutes (classes) from all five continents as well as from college and university teachers in China, making this the product of a multitude of people who show true interest in textbook compiling. We therefore want to extend our most sincere gratitude on behalf of the authors team to all those mentioned above. Although we put in all efforts and strived for the best, it is unavoidable that insufficiencies and inadequacies still exist, hence we would like to make a cordial request towards all teachers, students and readers who will use these books to present us their feedback at any time, so that we may continue to perfect them and make these books the best helper for learners of Chinese.

The Authors Team

July, 2021

本册编写说明

本册教材为《HSK 标准会话教程》系列教材的第二册，是中文学习的起步教程，适合掌握 150 个左右中文词语的在校学生及对中文感兴趣的社会人士等中文学习者使用。

本书词句难度等级依据汉语水平考试大纲二级（HSK 二级），用有限的词语和相对简单的语法规则生成尽可能多的交际句子，语句内容符合学习者的生活实际和认知水平。

另外，为了体现中文词汇的复合特点、充分利用 HSK 大纲词汇，本书在必要的时候也对大纲词语的构词语素进行了拆分利用，例如，大纲含“老师”和“机场”，本书用“老”和“机场”组合成新的短语“老机场”。

全书共 12 课，每一课建议授课时间为 2—3 课时，全书可以在 30—36 课时内完成。各课以赴华留学生学习和生活的亲身经历为主线串联起来，通过其学习和生活的轨迹不断地引入新的词汇和语法。

每一课都包含热身、课文、生词、语法点、练习和文化点六个部分。

热身部分采用独特的框架结构，将本课重点句式通过结构分解进行展示，用不同颜色、不同形状的图形显示不同位置上词语的功能，让句子的主体结构一目了然；用不同颜色、不同线型的线条连接成不同的句子，相同颜色的线条可以连成一个句子。同时对框内词语进行翻译，既能预习生词，还可以进行中英文句型的对照，使学习者了解中文短语的复合方法和句子的构成规则，从而培养典型语句的结构意识。

课文部分充分反映了会话教材的特点，包括两篇情景对话和一篇叙述性短文，将语言交际能力和个人陈述能力有机结合。两篇对话围绕本课重点语法和句型展开，旨在培养学习者在不同情境下运用同一个语法点进行口语交际的能力；一篇短文与对话内容相关，陈述事实，回顾一天发生的事情，相当于回答“今天做了什么”，目的是训练学习者的话语陈述能力和连贯表达能力。

生词部分按照惯例编排，列出了本课新出现的词语，提供了汉语拼音、词性说明和英文释义。

语法点部分用中英双语解释课文中出现的重点语法和词语，并给出仅用本级词语的典型例句，全书覆盖了 HSK 二级语法大纲的范围。

练习部分参考 HSK 二级和 HSKK 初级考试题型，对本课重点内容进行听说训练，有利于学习者熟悉考试题型，为顺利通过相应级别考试奠定基础。

文化点部分用中英双语介绍一则与本课内容相关的中国语言文化常识或当代中国国情，激发学习者兴趣，扩展其知识面，帮助其积累文化知识、理解中国语言文化。为减轻教材体量，这部分内容将作为网络资源提供给学习者。

本书语句紧扣 HSK 和 HSKK 大纲，内容清新，与时俱进，特色鲜明。初学者可以通过此书快速入门，体会中文学习的乐趣。千里之行，始于足下，让我们一起踏上中文学习之路吧！

编者

2021 年 8 月

A Guide to the Use of This Book

This volume is the second one in the *HSK Standard Conversational Course* series. It is an elementary course for learning Chinese, suitable for school students and other members of the broader community who have already grasped around 150 words in Chinese.

The difficulty level of the words and sentences in this book is based on the *HSK Test Syllabus* (HSK Level II). A limited number of words and expressions and fairly simple grammar rules have been used to generate a maximum amount of sentences true to life and tallying with learners' cognitive level.

Moreover, in order to exhibit the compounding nature of Chinese words and to make full use of the *HSK Vocabulary Outline*, when necessary, word-forming morphemes were split up and recombined into new phrases. For instance, the *Outline* contains the words 老师 and 机场, so in this book the morpheme 老 was paired up with 机场 to form a new phrase, 老机场.

This book contains 12 lessons in total. We suggest each lesson be taught for 2–3 hours, which brings the total amount of time for completing the whole book to 30–36 hours. The lessons are interconnected by a main storyline revolving around the personal experiences of international students living and studying in China, with new words and grammar points being constantly introduced by following their path of living and studying in China.

Each lesson comprises six sections, namely Warm-up, Texts, New Words, Language Points, Drills, and Cultural Aspects.

The Warm-up section utilizes a distinctive technique using boxes to break down key sentence structures and different colors and shapes to show how the function of words varies according to their position in the sentence, thus making the primary structure of a sentence become clear at a glance. Different colors and types of lines are used to connect different sentences, and lines with the same color can be connected to form a sentence. Moreover, the words in the boxes are translated so that learners may both prepare the new words in advance and compare Chinese sentence types with English ones, which helps them grasp the rules of compounding phrases and forming sentences in Chinese and become aware of typical sentence structures.

The Texts section fully reflects the qualities of a conversational textbook. This section consists of two situational dialogues and one narrative paragraph, which integrate discourse ability with individual narration ability. The two dialogues revolve around key grammar points and sentences from the lesson, intended to help nurture learners' ability to communicate using the same grammar points but under various contexts. The narrative paragraph is closely connected to the dialogues, mainly focusing on narrating facts, looking back at the day's events, basically answering the question "What did you do today?", with the purpose of training learners' ability of narrative discourse and coherent expression.

The New Words section employs a conventional layout, by listing the new words of each lesson along with the Pinyin, their part of speech and an English explanation.

The Language Points section uses both Chinese and English to explain the key grammar points and words and expressions which appear throughout the texts. These are complemented by typical illustrative sentences using words strictly corresponding to this level and covering the HSK Level Ⅱ grammar outline.

The Drills section is based on HSK Level Ⅱ and HSKK Primary Level question types. The purpose is to practice listening and speaking based on the main content of the lesson as well as to familiarize learners with actual HSK question types, so that they may have a basis for smoothly going through the test corresponding to their level.

The Cultural Aspects section introduces pieces of general knowledge regarding Chinese language and culture or the present situation in China, all in close connection with the content of the texts. This integration of language with culture captures learners' interests by expanding their scope of knowledge and helps them understand Chinese language and culture by accumulating cultural knowledge. This section will be put online in order to reduce the size of the printed textbook.

The words and sentences in this book are directly connected with the HSK and HSKK syllabi and are presented in a clear and distinctive content with up-to-date information. These features make this book a very good option for beginners to easily enter the world of learning Chinese and experience the joy that comes with it. A journey of a thousand miles begins with a single step, let us embark on the journey towards learning Chinese together!

The Author

August, 2021

目录 Contents

语法点
Language Points

语法点
Language Points

语法点
Language Points

1. 结果补语“完”：The complement of result “完”
2. “还可以”：The structure “还可以”
3. 形容词重叠“好好”：The reduplicated adjective “好好”
4. 表示时间晚的副词“就”：The adverb “就” indicating a late time
5. “就要……了”：The structure “就要……了”

书中主人公是两名在中国学习中文的留学生。书中内容以其在中国生活与学习的亲身经历为主线。

The main characters in the book are two international students studying Chinese in China. The stories in the book revolve around their personal experiences living and studying in China.

大卫，男，英国人，预科生，准备在中国一所大学读中国历史。

David, male, British, preparatory course student, preparing to study a major in Chinese History at a university in China.

莎莉，女，来自墨西哥，大卫的同学。

Sally, female, from Mexico, David's classmate.

另外，本书还有两个人经常出现在主人公的生活中。他们是：

In addition, there are two more people who often appear in the main characters' lives. They are:

尼克，男，美国人，在中国工作五年了，大卫的朋友。

Nick, male, American, working for five years in China, David's friend.

王华，女，大卫的中文老师。

Wang Hua, female, David's Chinese language teacher.

1 Lesson One

Wǒ gěi nín yì běn Zhōngwén shū ba

我给您一本中文书吧

Let me give you a Chinese language book

热身 Warm-up

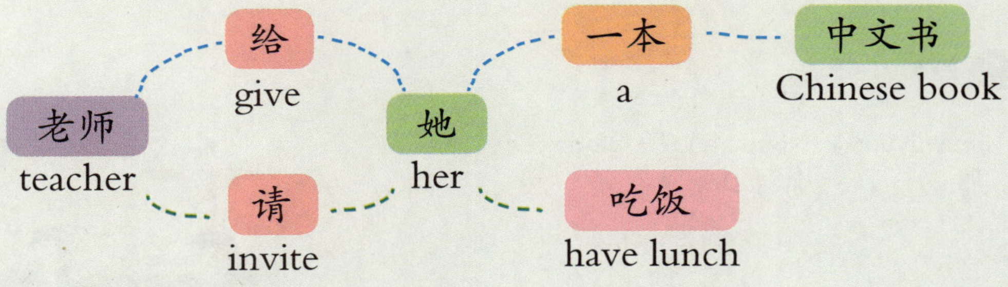

课文 Text

课文 1 01-1

Shālì māma: Wáng lǎoshī, zhè shì gěi nín de kāfēi, shì Mòxīgē zuì hǎo de kāfēi.
莎莉妈妈：王老师，这是给您的咖啡，是墨西哥最好的咖啡。

Wáng lǎoshī: Nín tài kèqi le. Wǒ gěi nín yì běn Zhōngwén shū ba.
王老师：您太客气了。我给您一本中文书吧。

Shālì māma: Xièxie nín. Wáng lǎoshī, wǒmen zhōngwǔ yìqǐ chī gè fàn ba.
莎莉妈妈：谢谢您。王老师，我们中午一起吃个饭吧。

Wáng lǎoshī: Hǎo a. Wǒ qǐng nǐmen chī fàn, huānyíng nín lái Běijīng.
王老师：好啊。我请你们吃饭，欢迎您来北京。

Text One

Sally's mom: Teacher Wang, this coffee is for you, it's the best Mexican coffee.
Teacher Wang: That's so nice of you. Let me give you a Chinese language book.
Sally's mom: Thank you. Teacher Wang, let's have lunch together.
Teacher Wang: Sure. I'll buy you two lunch to welcome you (Sally's mom) to Beijing.

课文 2 01-2

Fúwùyuán: Nǐmen hǎo! Qǐng wèn, nǐmen xiǎng chī shénme?
服务员：你们好！请问，你们想吃什么？

Wáng lǎoshī: Nǐmen zhèr zuì hǎochī de cài shì shénme? Qǐng gěi wǒmen jièshào yíxià.
王老师：你们这儿最好吃的菜是什么？请给我们介绍一下。

Fúwùyuán: Wǒmen zhèr de yú hé yángròu zuì hǎochī.
服务员：我们这儿的鱼和羊肉最好吃。

Wáng lǎoshī: Tài hǎo le. Shālì, nǐ xǐhuan chī shénme?
王老师：太好了。莎莉，你喜欢吃什么？

Shālì: Wǒ xǐhuan chī yú.
莎莉：我喜欢吃鱼。

Text Two

Waitress: Hello! What would you like to eat?
Teacher Wang: What's the best dish you have here? Please tell us a little bit about it.
Waitress: Our best dishes are the fish and the mutton.
Teacher Wang: Sounds great. Sally, what do you like to eat?
Sally: I like to eat fish.

课文 3 01-3

Jīntiān Shālì de māma lái xuéxiào le,
今天莎莉的妈妈来学校了，
tā gěile lǎoshī yìxiē kāfēi, lǎoshī gěile tā
她给了老师一些咖啡，老师给了她
yì běn Zhōngwén shū. Zhōngwǔ lǎoshī qǐng Shālì
一本中文书。中午老师请莎莉
hé tā māma qù fànguǎn chī fàn, tāmen yìqǐ chīle nàge fànguǎn zuì hǎochī de liǎng
和她妈妈去饭馆吃饭，她们一起吃了那个饭馆最好吃的两
gè cài yú hé yángròu.
个菜——鱼和羊肉。

Text Three

Sally's mom came to the school today, she gave the teacher some coffee and the teacher gave her a Chinese language book. At noon, the teacher invited Sally and her mom to have lunch at the restaurant, together they ate the best dishes at that restaurant, fish and mutton.

生词 New Words

给	gěi	v. / prep.	give; (*used after a verb*) to, for
咖啡	kāfēi	n.	coffee
最	zuì	adv.	most, to the greatest extent
客气	kèqi	adj.	polite
本	běn	m.	*used with books*
书	shū	n.	book
一起	yìqǐ	adv.	together
吧	ba	part.	*indicates a suggestion*

续表

欢迎	huānyíng	v.	to welcome
问	wèn	v.	to ask
鱼	yú	n.	fish
羊肉	yángròu	n.	mutton

语法点 Language Points

1 “给”：（1）动词，可以带两个宾语构成双宾语句。例如：

“给”：（1）Verb, which can take two objects to form a double object sentence. For example:

我给您一本中文书吧。

Let me give you a Chinese language book.

她给了老师一些咖啡。

She gave the teacher some coffee.

（2）介词，和名词或代词一起组成句子的状语，放在动词前。例如：

（2）Preposition, which forms the adverbial adjunct of the sentence along with a noun or a pronoun and is placed before the verb. For example:

请你给同学们介绍一下。

Please tell the class about it.

请给我们看一下这本书。

Please let us have a look at this book.

2 程度副词“最”：修饰形容词或心理动词，表示某一方面的最高程度。例如：

The adverb of degree“最”: used to modify adjectives or modal verbs. It expresses the highest degree of a certain aspect. For example:

这是墨西哥最好的咖啡。

This is the best Mexican coffee.

你们这儿最好吃的菜是什么？

What’s the best dish you have here?

我最喜欢吃羊肉。

I like to eat mutton best.

3 语气助词“吧”：用来表示商量、建议等，使语气更加委婉。例如：

The modal particle “吧”: used to soften the tone of a discussion, suggestion, etc. For example:

我给你妈妈一本中文书吧。

I’ll give your mom a Chinese language book.

我请你们喝茶吧。

Let me invite you to drink tea.

我们去饭馆吃吧。

Let’s eat at the restaurant.

4 动词 + 动量补语“一下”：“一下”是“介绍”的补语，因为这个补语表示动作、行为进行的数量、次数，所以叫作动量补语。“动词 + 一下”表示动作的轻、短或表示轻松的语气等。例如：

Verb+the complement of frequency “一下”: “一下” is the complement of the verb “介绍”. This complement is used to express the quantity or frequency of an action or behavior, therefore it is called a complement of frequency. The structure “verb + 一下” indicates a light and short action or a soft and relaxed tone. For example:

请给我们介绍一下。

Please tell us about it.

这是我写的书，您看一下。

This is a book I wrote, please have a look.

我是大卫，我们认识一下。

I’m David, let’s get to know each other.

练习 Drills

听力练习 Listening Drills

1 听词语，判断图片是否正确。 01–4

Listen to the words and determine whether the pictures are correct.

(1) ____ (2) ____ (3) ____ (4) ____ (5) ____

2 听句子，选择正确图片。 01–5
Listen to the sentences and choose the correct pictures.

（1）

A

B

C

（2）

A

B

C

（3）

A

B

C

（4）

A

B

C

（5）

A

B

C

3 听对话，选择正确图片。 01-6
Listen to the conversations and choose the correct pictures.

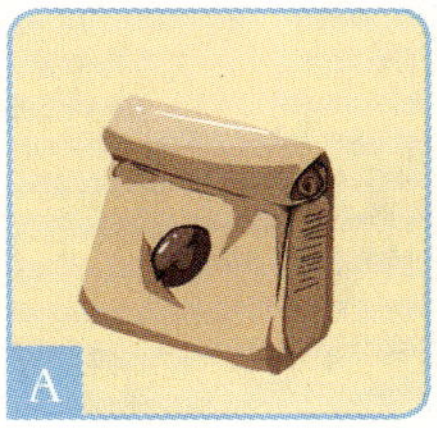
A

B

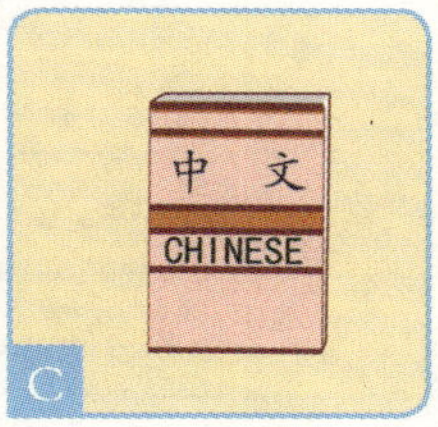

C

D

E

(1)		(2)	
(3)		(4)	
(5)			

4 听录音，选择正确答案。 01-7
Listen to the recordings and choose the correct answers.

(1)	A. māma 妈妈	B. lǎoshī 老师	C. wǒ 我	(　)
(2)	A. liǎng běn shū 两 本 书	B. kāfēi 咖啡	C. Zhōngwén shū 中 文 书	(　)
(3)	A. yú 鱼	B. yú hé yángròu 鱼和 羊 肉	C. yángròu 羊肉	(　)
(4)	A. fànguǎn 饭 馆	B. huí jiā 回 家	C. xuéxiào 学校	(　)
(5)	A. shāngdiàn 商 店	B. lǎoshī jiā 老师家	C. xuéxiào 学校	(　)

口语练习 Speaking Drills

5 听后重复。 01-8
Listen and repeat.

(1) ____________________

(2) ____________________

(3) ____________________

(4) ____________________

(5) ____________________

6 听后回答。 01-9

Listen and answer.

(1) ______________________

(2) ______________________

(3) ______________________

(4) ______________________

(5) ______________________

7 选词填空，读一读。

Fill in the blanks with the words and then read the text.

lái	qǐng	zuì	le	gěi
A. 来	B. 请	C. 最	D. 了	E. 给

Jīntiān Shālì de māma xuéxiào le, tā le lǎoshī yìxiē kāfēi, lǎoshī
今天莎莉的妈妈（　）学校了，她（　）了老师一些咖啡，老师（　）

tā yìběn Zhōngwén shū. Zhōngwǔ lǎoshī Shālì hé tā māma qù fànguǎn chī fàn, tāmen yìqǐ
她一本 中文 书。 中午 老师（　）莎莉和她妈妈去饭馆吃饭，她们一起

chī nàge fànguǎn hǎochī de yú hé yángròu.
吃（　）那个饭馆（　）好吃的鱼和 羊肉 。

Lesson Two

2 你的眼睛怎么红红的

Nǐ de yǎnjing zěnme hónghóng de

Why are your eyes so red

热身 Warm-up

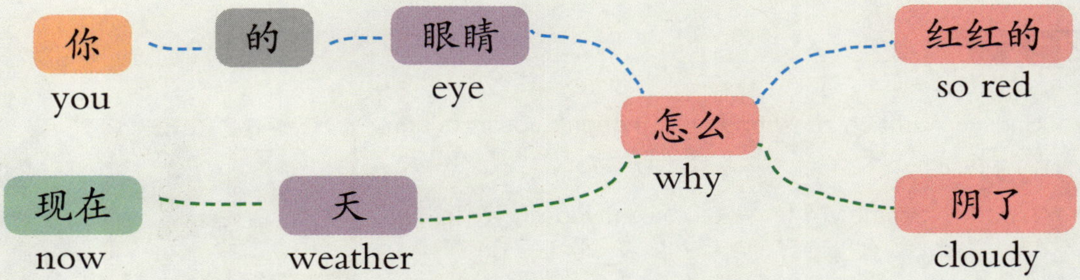

课文 Text

课文1 02-1

Dàwèi: Nǐ de yǎnjing zěnme hónghóng de?
大卫：你的眼睛怎么红红的？

Shālì: Yīnwèi wǒ zuótiān xuéxíle yì wǎnshang.
莎莉：因为我昨天学习了一晚上。

Dàwèi: Bú shì ba? Wǒ juéde shì yīnwèi nǐ māma jīntiān yào zǒu le, duì bú duì?
大卫：不是吧？我觉得是因为你妈妈今天要走了，对不对？

Shālì: Nǐ shuō de méi cuò.
莎莉：你说的没错。

Text One

David: Why are your eyes so red?

Sally: Because I was up studying all night.

David: It can't be, I think it's because your mom is leaving today, isn't that right?

Sally: You're right.

课文2 02-2

Shālì: Jīntiān zǎoshang shì qíngtiān, xiànzài tiān zěnme yīn le, shì bú shì yào xià yǔ le?
莎莉：今天早上是晴天，现在天怎么阴了，是不是要下雨了？

Dàwèi: Tiān yīn le, kěnéng yào xià yǔ, yě kěnéng yào xià xuě.
大卫：天阴了，可能要下雨，也可能要下雪。

Shālì: Xià xuě hǎo, wǒ xǐhuan xià xuě.
莎莉：下雪好，我喜欢下雪。

Dàwèi: Wǒ yě xǐhuan xià xuě.
大卫：我也喜欢下雪。

Text Two

Sally: It was clear this morning, how come it's turned cloudy now, is it going to rain?
David: It's become overcast, it might rain or it might snow.
Sally: Snow would be nice, I like it when it snows.
David: I like it when it snows, too.

课文 3 02-3

Shālì jīntiān zǎoshang lái xuéxiào shàngkè de shíhou, yǎnjing hónghóng de. Yīnwèi jīntiān tā māma zǒu le, tā yǒudiǎnr xiǎng māma.
莎莉今天早上来学校上课的时候，眼睛红红的。因为今天她妈妈走了，她有点儿想妈妈。

Xiàwǔ tiān yīn le, yǒudiǎnr lěng, bù zhīdào shì bú shì yào xià xuě. Wǒ hé Shālì dōu hěn xǐhuan xià xuě.
下午天阴了，有点儿冷，不知道是不是要下雪。我和莎莉都很喜欢下雪。

Text Three

When Sally came to class this morning, her eyes were very red. Her mom left today, so she misses her mom a little bit. In the afternoon, the sky became overcast and it was a bit cold. We don't know whether it's going to snow or not. Both Sally and I like it very much when it snows.

生词 New Words

眼睛	yǎnjing	n.	eye
红	hóng	adj.	red
因为	yīnwèi	conj.	because, as
晚上	wǎnshang	n.	evening, night
觉得	juéde	v.	to feel, to think
要	yào	aux.	to be about / going to, will
走	zǒu	v.	to leave, to walk
对	duì	adj.	right, correct

续表

错	cuò	adj.	wrong, incorrect
早上	zǎoshang	n.	morning
晴	qíng	adj.	sunny
阴	yīn	adj.	overcast, cloudy
可能	kěnéng	aux.	maybe, probably
也	yě	adv.	also, too
雪	xuě	n.	snow
上课	shàngkè	v.	to have a class
有点儿	yǒudiǎnr	adv.	a little
知道	zhīdào	v.	to know

语法点 Language Points

1 疑问代词“怎么”：是“为什么”的意思，“怎么＋动词/形容词”可以问原因，多带有惊讶、意外的语气。“怎么”可以用在主语前，也可以用在主语后。例如：

The interrogative pronoun“怎么”, meaning “how come” or “why”. The structure “怎么 +v. / adj.” can be used to inquire the reason when one is taken by surprise. “怎么” can be placed either before the subject or after the subject. For example:

你的眼睛怎么红红的？ ＝怎么你的眼睛红红的？

Why are your eyes so red?

怎么现在天阴了？ ＝现在天怎么阴了？

How come it's become overcast now?

你怎么不回家？ ＝怎么你不回家？

Why aren't you going back home?

2 形容词重叠：有些单音节形容词可以按 AA 式重叠，可以在句中作谓语，具有描写的作用。作谓语时，句末要有“的”。例如：

Reduplicated adjectives: some monosyllabic adjectives can be reduplicated according to the AA pattern in order to enhance their descriptive function. They can form the predicate of the sentence, in which case “的” should be used at the end of the sentence. For example:

现在天黑黑的。

The sky is very dark now.

她的眼睛红红的。

Her eyes are very red.

他女儿眼睛大大的。

His daughter's eyes are very big.

3 连词“因为”：用在分句的句首，表示原因。例如：

The conjunction “因为”: used at the beginning of a clause to indicate the reason. For example:

她喜欢北京，因为北京东西很便宜。

She likes Beijing, because things in Beijing are cheap.

我买了很多苹果，因为今天苹果很便宜。

I bought a lot of apples, because they are very cheap today.

老师今天没来学校，因为她生病了。

The teacher didn't come to school today, because she is sick.

4 语气助词“吧”：当说话人对情况有了某种估计，但又不能完全肯定时，可以在陈述句的句尾用“吧”构成疑问句，表示推测的意味。例如：

The modal particle “吧”: a speaker who reckons something but cannot be fully certain will use “吧” at the end of the sentence to form an interrogative sentence and to express an estimation. For example:

你是老师吧?

Are you a teacher?

A: 我昨天来上课了。

A: I came to class yesterday.

B: 不对吧? 我没看见你。

B: How can it be? I didn't see you.

A: 我昨天学习了一晚上。

A: I was up studying all night.

B: 不是吧?

B: Not really?

5 “要……了”：“要”是助动词，和“了”一起构成“要 + 动词 / 动词性短语 + 了”

的句式，表示动作将要发生。例如：

"要……了": "要" is an auxiliary verb used together with "了" to form the sentence pattern "要 + verb / phrasal verb +了 ", which expresses an action that is about to take place. For example:

我妈妈要回去了。

My mom will go back.

我要睡觉了。

I'm going to sleep.

快走吧，要上课了。

Let's hurry, class is about to start.

6 用"是不是""对不对"的正反疑问句：当说话人对情况有了比较肯定的估计时，为了进一步得到证实，就可以用"是不是""对不对"进行提问。"是不是"可以用在句首、句尾或谓语前，"对不对"只能放在句尾。例如：

Affirmative-negative questions with "是不是" and "对不对": when the speaker is fairly certain about their estimation, they may ask their question using "是不是" or "对不对" to obtain further confirmation. "是不是" can be used at the beginning of the sentence, at the end of the sentence, or in front of the predicate, whereas "对不对" can only be used at the end of the sentence. For example:

是不是要下雨了？

Isn't it going to rain?

你妈妈是不是要走了？

Your mom is about to leave, no?

你不高兴，是因为你妈妈要走了，对不对 / 是不是？

You're sad because your mom is going away, isn't that right?

当用"不知道"否定这个疑问句的时候，句子不再是疑问的语气，而是表示不确定的推测语气。例如：

When "不知道" is used to negate this type of affirmative-negative question, the sentence loses its interrogative tone and only expresses an uncertain feeling about a situation. For example:

不知道是不是要下雨。

I'm not sure whether it's going to rain or not.

他今天没来学校，不知道是不是生病了。

He didn't come to school today, I'm wondering whether he's sick.

练习 Drills

听力练习 Listening Drills

1 听词语，判断图片是否正确。 02-4
Listen to the words and determine whether the pictures are correct.

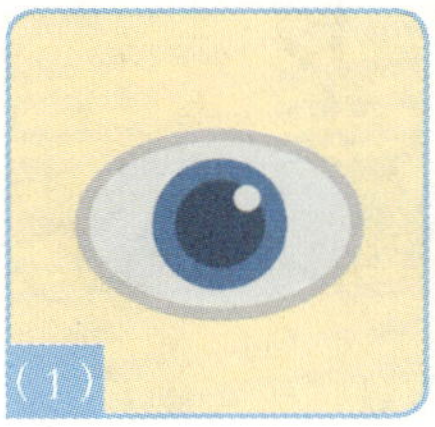
(1) ______

(2) ______

(3) ______

(4) ______

(5) ______

2 听句子，选择正确图片。 02-5
Listen to the sentences and choose the correct pictures.

(1)

A

B

C

(2)

A

B

C

(3)

A

B

C

（4）

A

B

C

（5）

A

B

C

3 听对话，选择正确图片。 02-6

Listen to the conversations and choose the correct pictures.

A

B

C

D

E

（1）		（2）	
（3）		（4）	
（5）			

4 听录音，选择正确的答案。 02-7

Listen to the recordings and choose the correct answers.

	A	B	C	
（1）	A. dàdà de 大大的	B. hónghóng de 红红的	C. hēihēi de 黑黑的	（　）
（2）	A. Běijīng 北京	B. jīchǎng 机场	C. huí jiā 回家	（　）
（3）	A. xiǎng māma 想妈妈	B. xiǎng xuéxí 想学习	C. xiǎng chī fàn 想吃饭	（　）
（4）	A. qíng 晴	B. yīn 阴	C. lěng 冷	（　）
（5）	A. xià yǔ 下雨	B. qíng tiān 晴天	C. xià xuě 下雪	（　）

口语练习 Speaking Drills

5 听后重复。 02–8

Listen and repeat.

（1）______

（2）______

（3）______

（4）______

（5）______

6 听后回答。 02–9

Listen and answer.

（1）______

（2）______

（3）______

（4）______

（5）______

7 回答问题。

Answer the question.

Shuōshuo jīntiān de tiānqì.
说 说 今天 的 天气。

______

______

3 Lesson Three

Xuě zhèngzài xià ne

雪正在下呢

It's snowing right now

热身 Warm-up

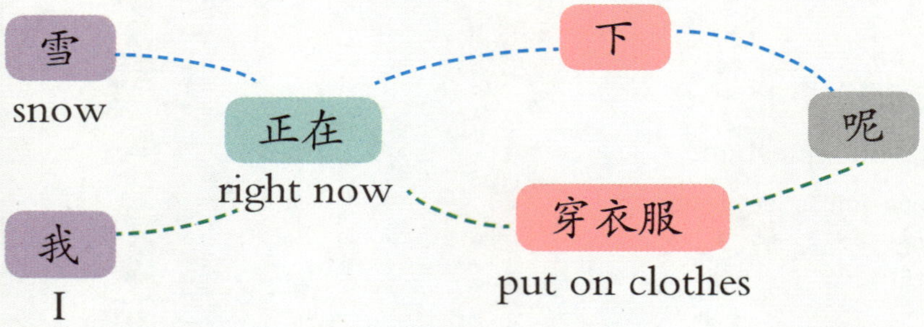

课文 Text

课文 1 03-1

Shālì: Dàwèi, nǐ hái zài shuìjiào ma? Nǐ qǐchuángle ma?
莎莉：大卫，你还在睡觉吗？你起床了吗？

Dàwèi: Wǒ qǐchuáng le. Zěnme le?
大卫：我起床了。怎么了？

Shālì: Zhēn de xià xuě le, fēicháng piàoliang. Nǐ kuài chūlái yìqǐ wánr ba. Xuě zhèngzài xià ne.
莎莉：真的下雪了，非常漂亮。你快出来一起玩儿吧。雪正在下呢。

Dàwèi: Tài hǎo le! Děng wǒ jǐ fēnzhōng, wǒ zhèngzài chī fàn ne.
大卫：太好了！等我几分钟，我正在吃饭呢。

Text One

Sally: David, are you still sleeping? Are you up?

David: I'm up. What's up?

Sally: It's really snowing, it's very beautiful. Hurry and come out, let's enjoy it together. It's snowing.

David: That's great! Give me a few minutes, I'm eating right now.

课文 2 03-2

Shālì: Dōu bàn gè xiǎoshí le, nǐ zěnme hái méi chūlái?
莎莉：都半个小时了，你怎么还没出来？

Dàwèi: Zài děng liǎng fēnzhōng, wǒ zhèngzài chuān yīfu ne.
大卫：再等两分钟，我正在穿衣服呢。

Shālì: Wǒ zài fànguǎn qiánmiàn děng nǐ.
莎莉：我在饭馆前面等你。

Dàwèi: Hǎo de. Wǒ yǐjīng chūmén le.
大卫：好的。我已经出门了。

Text Two

Sally: It's already been half an hour, why are you still not coming out?

David: Give me two more minutes, I'm putting on my clothes right now.

Sally: I'm waiting for you in front of the restaurant.

David: OK. I'm out now.

课文 3 02–3

Jīntiān zǎoshang, wǒ zhèngzài chī dōngxi de shíhou, Shālì gàosu wǒ xià xuě le. Zhè shì wǒ dì-èr cì kànjiàn xuě, dì-yī cì shì wǒ qī-bā suì de shíhou. Zhè shì Shālì dì-yī cì kànjiàn xuě, tā fēicháng gāoxìng. Wǒmen yìqǐ zuòle yí gè xuěrén.

今天早上，我正在吃东西的时候，莎莉告诉我下雪了。这是我第二次看见雪，第一次是我七八岁的时候。这是莎莉第一次看见雪，她非常高兴。我们一起做了一个雪人。

Text Three

When I was eating this morning, Sally told me that it snowed today. This was the second time for me to see snow, the first time was when I was about seven or eight years old. It's the first time for Sally to see snow. She was very excited. We made a snowman together.

生词 New Words

还	hái	adv.	still, in addition
起床	qǐchuáng	v.	to get out of bed, to get up
真的	zhēn de	adv.	really
快	kuài	adj.	fast, quick
出（来）	chū (lái)	v.	to come out, to get out
玩	wán	v.	to play
等	děng	v.	to wait
正在	zhèngzài	adv.	right now, in the process / course of
半	bàn	num.	half
小时	xiǎoshí	n.	hour

续表

再	zài	adv.	again, once more
穿	chuān	v.	(of clothes) to wear, to put on
已经	yǐjīng	adv.	already
门	mén	n.	door
告诉	gàosu	v.	to tell
第二	dì-èr	num.	second
次	cì	m.	*indicates the number of times sth. is done or experienced*
第一	dì-yī	num.	first
非常	fēicháng	adv.	very, extremely
雪人	xuěrén	n.	snowman

语法点 Language Points

1 语气副词"还"：意思是"仍旧""依然"，表示动作继续进行或状况继续存在。否定词"不"或"没"放在"还"后面。例如：

The modal adverb "还": meaning "still" "yet" "as before", used to express that the action continues, or that the situation still exists. Negation words ("不"or"没") are placed after "还". For example:

你还在睡觉吗？

Are you still sleeping?

九点了，他还没起床。

It's (already) nine o'clock, he's still not up.

你还不去学校吗？

You're not going to school yet?

2 副词"正在"：强调在某个时间点上动作的进行状态，句尾可以加"呢"表示肯定的语气。例如：

The adverb "正在": used to emphasize that an action is taking place right at a specific time. It can be accompanied by "呢" at the end of the sentence for further affirmation. For example:

尼克回家的时候，女儿正在睡觉呢。

When Nick got back home, his daughter was sleeping.

我到教室的时候，他正在看书呢。

As I entered the classroom, he was there reading.

我去看电影的时候，他正在学习呢。

While I went to see a movie, he was studying.

3 “都……了”：“都”表示“已经”的意思，轻读，和句尾的“了”一起构成“都……了”的句式。在“都……了”中间嵌套的部分是说话人要强调的重点，强调时间长、数量大、动作早、情况特别等。例如：

“都……了”: in this sentence pattern, “都” means “already” and is pronounced in a neutral tone, and “了” is placed at the end of the sentence. The content within “都……了” should be the point the speaker wants to emphasize, such as a long time, a large number, an early action, or a special situation. For example:

我都来了一个月了。

I’ve already been here one month.

现在苹果都20块钱一公斤了。

Apples cost 20 yuan per kilo now.

她都工作了三年了。

She’s been working for three years.

4 副词“再”：表示动作的重复或继续。这个动作是还没有发生的。例如：

The adverb “再”: expresses the repetition or continuation of an action which hasn’t taken place yet. For example:

我明天再来。

I’ll come back again tomorrow.

我想再去商店买一个杯子。

I want to go to the store again to buy a cup.

再等两分钟。

Wait two more minutes.

5 前缀“第”：用在整数的数词的前面，表示次序。例如：

The prefix “第”: used in front of a numeral to show the order or sequence. For example:

这是我第二次看见雪。

This is the second time I’ve seen snow.

今天是我来北京的第一天。

This is my first day in Beijing.

今天我们学习第五课。

Today we will study the fifth lesson.

练习 Drills

听力练习 Listening Drills

1 听词语，判断图片是否正确。 03–4

Listen to the words and determine whether the pictures are correct.

(1)

(2)

(3)
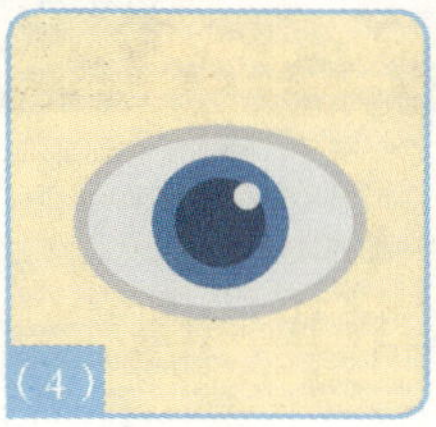
(4)

(5)

______ ______ ______ ______ ______

2 听句子，选择正确图片。 03–5

Listen to the sentences and choose the correct pictures.

（1）

A

B

C

（2）

A

B

C

（3）

A

B

C

（4）

A

B

C

（5）

A

B

C

3 听对话，选择正确图片。 03–6

Listen to the conversations and choose the correct pictures.

（1）		（2）	
（3）		（4）	
（5）			

4 听录音，选择正确答案。 03–7

Listen to the recordings and choose the correct answers.

（1）A. 起床 qǐchuáng　B. 吃饭 chī fàn　C. 睡觉 shuìjiào　（　）

（2）A. 下雪 xià xuě　B. 下雨 xià yǔ　C. 很冷 hěn lěng　（　）

（3）A. 第一次 dì-yī cì　B. 第二次 dì-èr cì　C. 第三次 dì-sān cì　（　）

（4）A. 早上 zǎoshang　B. 中午 zhōngwǔ　C. 下午 xiàwǔ　（　）

（5）A. 饭馆前面 fànguǎn qiánmiàn　B. 饭馆后面 fànguǎn hòumiàn　C. 饭馆里 fànguǎn li　（　）

口语练习 Speaking Drills

5 听后重复。 03-8
Listen and repeat.

（1）______
（2）______
（3）______
（4）______
（5）______

6 听后回答。 03-9
Listen and answer.

（1）______
（2）______
（3）______
（4）______
（5）______

7 回答问题。
Answer the question.

Nǐ jiā nàli xià xuě ma?
你家那里下雪吗？

______
______

Lesson Four

4 你的足球踢得真好

Nǐ de zúqiú tī de zhēn hǎo

You play football really well

热身 Warm-up

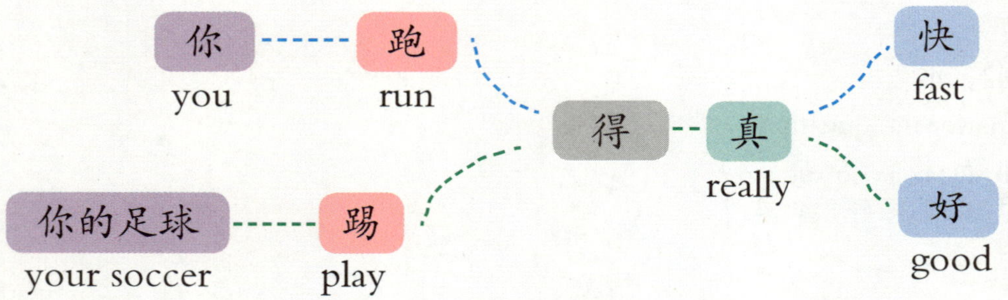

课文 Text

课文 1 04-1

Dàwèi: Nǐ pǎo de zhēn kuài. Nǐ tiāntiān dōu pǎobù ma?
大卫：你跑得真快。你天天都跑步吗？

Shālì: Shì de, wǒ měitiān pǎo sānshí fēnzhōng.
莎莉：是的，我每天跑三十分钟。

Dàwèi: Nǐ shì cóng shénme shíhou kāishǐ pǎobù de?
大卫：你是从什么时候开始跑步的？

Shālì: Wǒ cóng shí suì kāishǐ tiāntiān pǎobù, yǐjīng pǎole bā-jiǔ nián le.
莎莉：我从十岁开始天天跑步，已经跑了八九年了。

Text One

David: You run really fast. Do you run every day?

Sally: Yes, I run for thirty minutes every day.

David: When did you start running?

Sally: I started running when I was ten years old, I've been running for eight or nine years now.

课文 2 04-2

Shālì: Nǐ de zúqiú tī de zhēnhǎo.
莎莉：你的足球踢得真好。

Dàwèi: Nǐ kěnéng bù zhīdào, wǒ cóng bā suì kāishǐ tī zúqiú, yǐjīng tīle shí duō nián le.
大卫：你可能不知道，我从八岁开始踢足球，已经踢了十多年了。

Shālì: Nǐ hái xǐhuan shénme yùndòng?
莎莉：你还喜欢什么运动？

Dàwèi: Wǒ hái xǐhuan dǎ lánqiú hé yóuyǒng, dànshì lánqiú dǎ de bù hǎo.
大卫：我还喜欢打篮球和游泳，但是篮球打得不好。

Text Two

Sally: You play football really well.

David: Maybe you don't know, but I started playing football when I was eight years old, so I've been playing it for more than ten years now.

Sally: What other sports do you like?

David: I also like basketball and swimming, but I don't play basketball very well.

课文 3 04–3

Wǒ hé Shālì dōu xǐhuan yùndòng.
我和莎莉都喜欢运动。

Wǒ xǐhuan tī zúqiú, dǎ lánqiú hé yóuyǒng,
我喜欢踢足球、打篮球和游泳，

Shālì xǐhuan pǎobù. Shālì cóng shí suì kāishǐ
莎莉喜欢跑步。莎莉从十岁开始

tiāntiān zǎoshang pǎobù, dào xiànzài yǐjīng pǎole bā-jiǔ nián le. Wǒ cóng bā suì
天天早上跑步，到现在已经跑了八九年了。我从八岁

kāishǐ tī zúqiú, dào xiànzài yě yǐjīng tīle shí duō nián le.
开始踢足球，到现在也已经踢了十多年了。

Text Three

Both Sally and I like sports. I like playing football, basketball and swimming, Sally likes running. Sally has been running every morning since she was ten years old, it's been eight or nine years now. I started playing football when I was eight years old, so I've been playing it for more than ten years now.

生词 New Words

跑	pǎo	v.	to run
得	de	part.	*indicates the result or degree*
真	zhēn	adv.	really, indeed
每	měi	pron.	every
从	cóng	prep.	from
开始	kāishǐ	v.	to begin, to start
跑步	pǎobù	v. / n.	to run; running

续表

足球	zúqiú	n.	soccer, football
踢（足球）	tī (zúqiú)	v.	to play (soccer)
运动	yùndòng	n. / v.	sports; to exercise
打（篮球）	dǎ (lánqiú)	v.	to play (basketball)
游泳	yóuyǒng	v.	to swim
但是	dànshì	conj.	but, however
篮球	lánqiú	n.	basketball
到	dào	v.	to arrive, to reach, to get to

语法点 Language Points

1 情态补语“得”：动词后可以用“得”连接一个补充说明动作状态的成分，这种成分叫情态补语。例如：

The complement of state “得”: It is placed after the verb to connect it to a component that further explains the state of the action; this component is called a complement of state. For example:

你跑得真快。

You run really fast.

他走得很慢。

He walks very slowly.

如果动词有支配对象，可以重复动词，构成“动词 + 宾语 + 动词 + 得”的句式。例如：

If the verb is paired with an object, it can be duplicated to form the “verb + object + verb + 得” sentence pattern. For example:

你踢足球踢得真好。

You play football really well.

他说中文说得很好。

He speaks Chinese really well.

也可以省略第一个重复的动词。例如：

Or the first verb in the duplicated pattern may be omitted. For example:

你足球踢得真好。

You play football really well.

他中文说得很好。

He speaks Chinese really well.

还可以在主语后加“的”。例如：

Also, “ 的 ” may be added after the subject. For example:

你的足球踢得真好。

You play football really well.

他的汉语说得很好。

He speaks Chinese really well.

2 程度副词“真”：后面加形容词后可以一起作句子的补语和谓语，表示比较高、比较深的程度或感叹、夸张，但不能作定语和状语。例如：

The adverb of degree “真”: followed by an adjective to form the complement or predicate of the sentence, which expresses a high degree of something or a strong exclamation. It cannot serve as an attributive or adverbial adjunct. For example:

他跑得真快！

He runs really fast!

他足球踢得真好！

He plays football so well!

今天天气真好！

The weather is so nice today!

3 介词“从”：可以表示时间的起点，后面跟表示时间的词语，也可以跟表示时间终点的“到”搭配使用。例如：

The preposition “从”: used to indicate the starting point of a specific time. It is followed by words that express time and can also collocate with “ 到 ” to show the end point of a specific time. For example:

我从十岁开始跑步。

I started running when I was ten years old.

我从明天开始准备考试。

I will start preparing for my exams (from) tomorrow.

大卫从八岁开始踢足球，到现在已经快十年了。

David started playing football when he was eight years old, it’s been almost ten years (until) now.

4 转折连词“但是”：表示前后两个分句之间的转折关系，“但是”后面的内容是句子的重点。例如：

The transitional conjunction “但是”: indicates a transition between two clauses. The content following “但是” is the main point of the sentence. For example:

我喜欢打篮球，但是打得不好。

I like playing basketball, but I don’t play it well.

我想去看电影，但是没时间。

I want to see a movie, but I don’t have time.

他想买一件衣服，但是没钱买。

He wants to buy a garment, but doesn’t have the money to buy it.

5 量词重叠：是通过重叠以及读作重音的方式来强调没有例外。例如：

Reduplicated measure words: When a measure word is reduplicated and stressed in pronunciation, it means “every / each” and is used to indicate that there is no exception. For example:

我天天跑步。

I run every day.

这些衣服件件漂亮。

Each and every one of these clothes looks nice.

同学们个个都喜欢打篮球。

All of the students like to play basketball.

练习 Drills

听力练习 Listening Drills

1 听词语，判断图片是否正确。 04-4

Listen to the words and determine whether the pictures are correct.

(1)

(2)

(3)

(4)

(5)

____ ____ ____ ____ ____

2 听句子，选择正确图片。 04-5

Listen to the sentences and choose the correct pictures.

(1)

A

B

C

(2)

A

B

C

(3)

A

B

C

(4)

A

B

C

(5)

A

B

C

3 听对话，选择正确图片。 04–6

Listen to the conversations and choose the correct pictures.

A

B

C

D

E

(1)		(2)	
(3)		(4)	
(5)			

4 听录音，选择正确答案。 04–7

Listen to the recordings and choose the correct answers.

	A	B	C	
(1)	A. yóuyǒng 游泳	B. pǎobù 跑步	C. tī zúqiú 踢足球	(　　)
(2)	A. tī zúqiú 踢足球	B. dǎ lánqiú 打篮球	C. yóuyǒng 游泳	(　　)
(3)	A. qī suì 七岁	B. shí-yī suì 十一岁	C. shí suì 十岁	(　　)
(4)	A. pǎobù 跑步	B. dǎ lánqiú 打篮球	C. yóuyǒng 游泳	(　　)
(5)	A. gèzi gāo 个子高	B. tī zúqiú 踢足球	C. dǎ lánqiú 打篮球	(　　)

口语练习 Speaking Drills

5 听后重复。 04–8

Listen and repeat.

(1) ______________________

(2) ______________________

(3) ______________________

(4) ______________________

(5) ______________________

6 听后回答。 04-9

Listen and answer.

(1) ____________________

(2) ____________________

(3) ____________________

(4) ____________________

(5) ____________________

7 回答问题。

Answer the question.

Shuōshuo nǐ xǐhuan de yùndòng .
说说 你 喜欢 的 运 动 。

____

____

5 Lesson Five

Zhōngwǔ shuìjiào duì shēntǐ hǎo

中午睡觉对身体好

Napping at noon is good for our health

热身 Warm-up

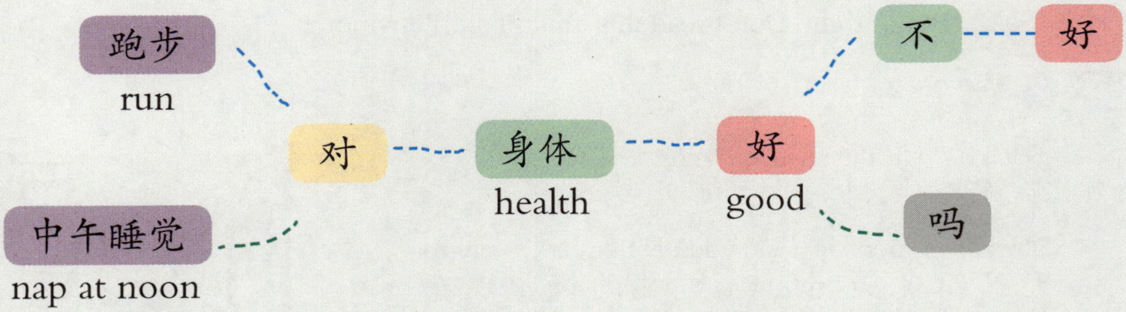

课文 Text

课文1 05-1

Dàwèi: Zuótiān wǒ kàn bào shang shuō, tiāntiān pǎobù duì shēntǐ bù hǎo, nǐ bié zài pǎobù le.
大卫：昨天我看报上说，天天跑步对身体不好，你别再跑步了。

Shālì: Zhēn de? Nǐ kàn de shì shénme bàozhǐ?
莎莉：真的？你看的是什么报纸？

Dàwèi: Wǒ shì zài shǒujī shang kàn de.
大卫：我是在手机上看的。

Shālì: Tā shuō de búduì. Nǐ bié zài kàn zhèxiē dōngxi le.
莎莉：它说的不对。你别再看这些东西了。

Text One

David: I read in the newspaper yesterday that running every day isn't good for our health, don't run anymore.

Sally: Really? What newspaper did you read?

David: I read it on the phone.

Sally: It's not right. Don't read this kind of stuff anymore.

课文2 05-2

Shālì: Nǐ zhōngwǔ qù nǎr chī fàn?
莎莉：你中午去哪儿吃饭？

Dàwèi: Wǒ shì shí diǎn duō chī de fàn, xiànzài wǒ yǒudiǎnr lèi le, xiǎng huí jiā shuì yí jiào. Dàjiā dōu shuō zhōngwǔ shuìjiào duì shēntǐ hǎo.
大卫：我是十点多吃的饭，现在我有点儿累了，想回家睡一觉。大家都说中午睡觉对身体好。

Shālì: Shì de, wǒ de hěn duō Zhōngguó péngyou dōu xǐhuan shuì wǔjiào.
莎莉：是的，我的很多中国朋友都喜欢睡午觉。

Dàwèi: Nǐ shuì wǔjiào ma?
大卫：你睡午觉吗？

Shālì: Wǒ yǒu shíhou yě shuì.
莎莉：我有时候也睡。

Text Two

Sally: Where are you going for lunch at noon?

David: It was past ten when I ate, I'm a bit tired now, so I want to go back home to take a nap. Everyone says sleeping at noon is good for our health.

Sally: That's right, many of my Chinese friends like to take naps at noon.

David: Do you take noon naps?

Sally: I also do sometimes.

课文 3 05-3

Yǒu de bàozhǐ shuō měitiān duō shuìjiào duì shēntǐ hǎo, yǒu de bàozhǐ shuō měitiān bú yào shuì de tài duō, shuì de tài duō le duì shēntǐ bù hǎo, zhēn bù zhīdào shéi shuō de duì. Wǒ juéde zhōngwǔ shuì yíhuìr jiào duì shēntǐ hěn hǎo.

有的报纸说每天多睡觉对身体好，有的报纸说每天不要睡得太多，睡得太多了对身体不好，真不知道谁说的对。我觉得中午睡一会儿觉对身体很好。

Text Three

Some newspapers say that sleeping more every day is good for our health, others say that we shouldn't sleep too much because it's bad for our health, I really don't know who's right. I think sleeping a little bit at noon is good for our health.

生词 New Words

对	duì	prep.	to, for
身体	shēntǐ	n.	body
报纸	bàozhǐ	n.	newspaper
手机	shǒujī	n.	cellphone
它	tā	pron.	it
别	bié	adv.	do not
累	lèi	adj.	tired

续表

睡	shuì	v.	to sleep, to nap
大家	dàjiā	pron.	everybody, everyone
午觉	wǔjiào	n.	noontime nap
有时候	yǒu shíhou		sometimes
不要	bú yào	adv.	do not
一会儿	yíhuìr	num.	a little while

语法点 Language Points

1 A对B(不)好：用“对”提示A和B之间的关系，A行为是否影响B。例如：

A is (not) good for B: “对” is used to indicate the relationship between A and B, whether the actions of A influence B or not. For example:

喝茶对身体好。

Drinking tea is good for your health.

在黑黑的房间里看手机对眼睛不好。

Looking at your phone in a room with no light is bad for your eyes.

跑步对身体好不好？

Is running good for our health?

2 “别……了”：“别”是否定副词，意思是“不”，可以和“了”构成表示命令或请求的句子。例如：

“别……了”: “别” is an adverb of negation meaning “don’t”. It is used together with “了” to form sentences expressing an order or a request. For example:

别吃了。

Don’t eat it.

别说了。

Stop saying (that).

别再看这些东西了。

Don’t read this kind of stuff anymore.

3 “的”字短语：动词可以加“的”构成“的”字短语，其功能相当于一个名词，可以作主语和宾语。例如：

The 的-phrase: verbs can be paired with “的” to form the 的-phrase, which acts just like a noun and can serve as a subject or an object. For example:

莎莉说的没错。

What Sally said is right.

你看的是什么报纸？

What's the newspaper you read?

你给的不是我想要的。

What you gave me is not what I wanted.

4 “睡一觉”：“睡觉”中间可以插入其他成分，如“一”“个”“一会儿”“一个小时”等。例如：

“睡一觉”: other components may be added in the middle of “睡觉”, like “一” “个” “一会儿” “一个小时”, etc. For example:

我有点儿累了，中午想回家睡一觉。

I'm a bit tired, I want to go back home at noon to take a nap.

他每天中午都睡一个小时觉。

He sleeps for one hour every day at noon.

中午睡一会儿觉对身体好。

Sleeping a little bit at noon is good for our health.

5 连词“所以”：可以和“因为”构成一组表示因果关系的关联词，把两个在意义上有因果关系的句子组合在一起，构成因果关系的复句。表示原因的分句在前面时，“因为”可以省略。例如：

The causal conjuction “所以”: “所以” and “因为” form a pair of connectors which indicate cause and effect. They connect two sentences which semantically have a cause and effect relationship and turn them into cause and effect clauses. If the clause containing the cause is in the front, “因为” may be omitted. For example:

（因为）公司的人不多，所以非常忙。

(Because) there aren't many people working at the company, (so) I'm very busy.

（因为）我喜欢学习中文，所以我来到了中国。

(Because) I like learning Chinese, (so) I came to China.

（因为）这件衣服很便宜，所以我买了两件。

(Because) this garment is very cheap, (so) I bought two pieces.

练习 Drills

听力练习 Listening Drills

1 听词语，判断图片是否正确。 05-4
Listen to the words and determine whether the pictures are correct.

(1) ______

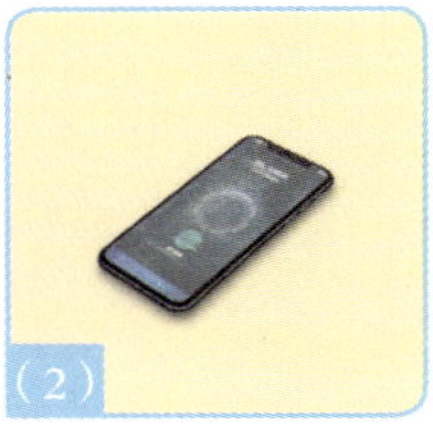
(2) ______

(3) ______

(4) ______

(5) ______

2 听句子，选择正确图片。 05-5
Listen to the sentences and choose the correct pictures.

(1)

A

B

C

(2)

A

B

C

(3)

A

B

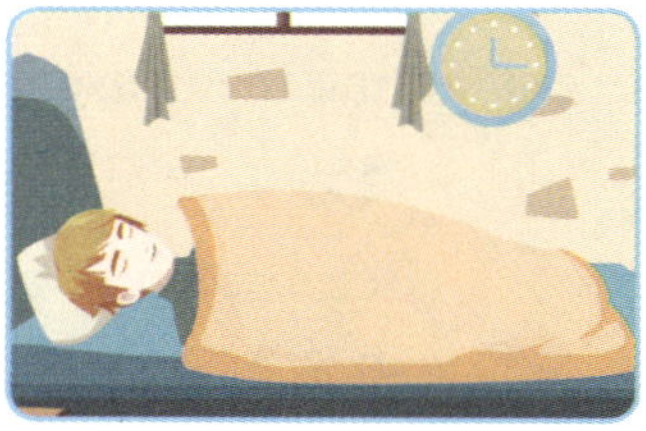
C

（4）

A

B

C

（5）

A

B

C

3 听对话，选择正确图片。 05–6

Listen to the conversations and choose the correct pictures.

A

B

C

D

E

（1）		（2）	
（3）		（4）	
（5）			

4 听录音，选择正确答案。 05–7

Listen to the recordings and choose the correct answers.

（1）A. 好 (hǎo)　　B. 不好 (bù hǎo)　　C. 身体 (shēntǐ)　　（　　）

（2）A. 对 (duì)　　B. 不对 (bú duì)　　C. 不 知道 (bù zhīdào)　　（　　）

（3）A. 冷 (lěng)　　B. 热 (rè)　　C. 累 (lèi)　　（　　）

（4）A. 学 校 (xuéxiào)　　B. 家 (jiā)　　C. 跑步 (pǎobù)　　（　　）

（5）A. 房 间 (fángjiān)　　B. 学 校 (xuéxiào)　　C. 教室 (jiàoshì)　　（　　）

口语练习 Speaking Drills

5 听后重复。 05–8
Listen and repeat.

(1) ____________________

(2) ____________________

(3) ____________________

(4) ____________________

(5) ____________________

6 听后回答。 05–9
Listen and answer.

(1) ____________________

(2) ____________________

(3) ____________________

(4) ____________________

(5) ____________________

7 回答问题。
Answer the question.

Nǐ juéde shuì wǔjiào duì shēntǐ hǎo ma ?
你 觉得 睡 午觉 对 身体 好 吗?

____

____

6 Lesson Six

Xīn jīchǎng bǐ lǎo jīchǎng hǎo

新机场比老机场好

The new airport is better than the old one

热身 Warm-up

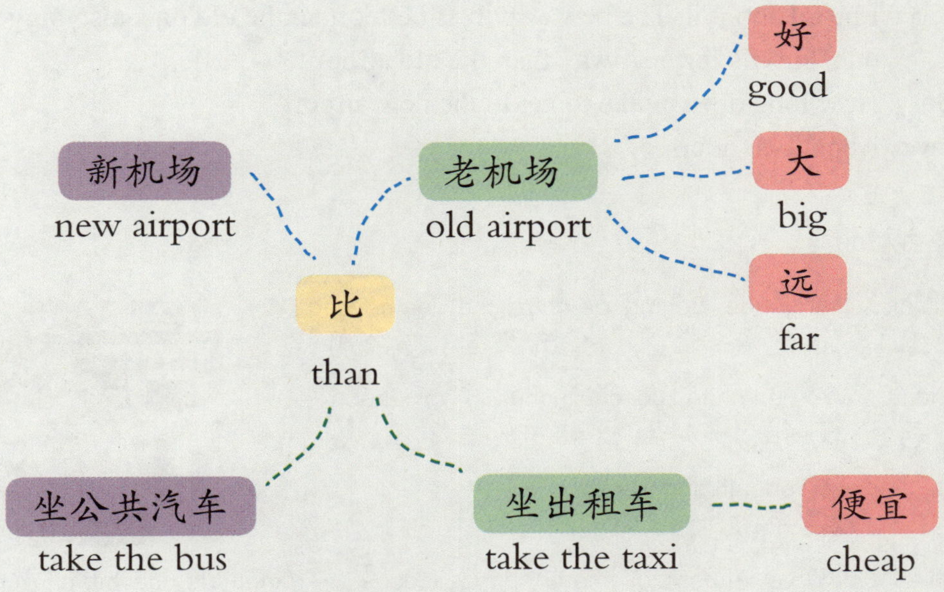

课文 Text

课文 1 06-1

Shālì: Nǐ zhīdào ma? Běijīng yǒu xīn jīchǎng le.
莎莉：你知道吗？北京有新机场了。

Dàwèi: Wǒ tīngshuō le. Xīn jīchǎng bǐ lǎo jīchǎng hǎo, yě bǐ lǎo jīchǎng dà, dànshì bǐ lǎo jīchǎng yuǎn.
大卫：我听说了。新机场比老机场好，也比老机场大，但是比老机场远。

Shālì: Dào xīn jīchǎng yào duō cháng shíjiān?
莎莉：到新机场要多长时间？

Dàwèi: Kěnéng yào liǎng gè xiǎoshí.
大卫：可能要两个小时。

Text One

Sally: Did you know? There's a new airport in Beijing.

David: I heard about it. The new airport is better than the old one, also bigger than the old one, but it's further away than the old airport.

Sally: How long does it take to get to the new airport?

David: About two hours.

课文 2 06-2

Dàwèi: Nǐ juéde Běijīng de chūzūchē zěnmeyàng?
大卫：你觉得北京的出租车怎么样？

Shālì: Wǒ hěn shǎo zuò chūzūchē, wǒ xǐhuan zài shǒujī shang jiàochē.
莎莉：我很少坐出租车，我喜欢在手机上叫车。

Dàwèi: Wǒ yě xǐhuan zài shǒujī shang jiàochē, tāmen de chē bǐ chūzūchē hǎo, chēqián yě bù bǐ chūzūchē guì.
大卫：我也喜欢在手机上叫车，他们的车比出租车好，车钱也不比出租车贵。

Shālì: Shì de, hái kěyǐ děng chē láile zài chūmén.
莎莉：是的，还可以等车来了再出门。

Text One

David: What do you think about the taxis in Beijing?

Sally: I seldom take taxis, I prefer to call for a car on my phone.

David: I also like to call for cars on my phone, they're better than taxis and the fares aren't more expensive than taxi fares.

Sally: Yes, and you can also wait until the car has arrived before getting out the house.

课文 3 06-3

Tīngshuō Běijīng yǒu xīn jīchǎng le. Xīn jīchǎng
听说北京有新机场了。新机场
bǐ lǎo jīchǎng hǎo, dànshì bǐ lǎo jīchǎng yuǎn.
比老机场好，但是比老机场远。
Cóng xuéxiào dào xīn jīchǎng kěyǐ zuò chūzūchē,
从学校到新机场可以坐出租车，
yě kěyǐ zuò gōnggòng qìchē hé dìtiě. Zuò chūzūchē kěnéng yào èrbǎi kuài qián,
也可以坐公共汽车和地铁。坐出租车可能要二百块钱，
zuò gōnggòng qìchē hé dìtiě bǐ zuò chūzūchē piányi.
坐公共汽车和地铁比坐出租车便宜。

Text Three

I heard that there's a new airport in Beijing. The new airport is better than the old one, but it's further away than the old airport. You can get to the new airport from the school by taxi or by bus and subway. Taking a taxi costs around two hundred yuan, taking the bus and the subway is cheaper than taking a taxi.

生词 New Words

新	xīn	adj.	new
机场	jīchǎng	n.	airport
听说	tīngshuō	v.	to hear, to learn about, to be told
比	bǐ	prep.	than
老	lǎo	adj.	old
远	yuǎn	adj.	far
要	yào	aux.	should, have to

续表

长	cháng	adj.	long
时间	shíjiān	n.	time
出租车	chūzūchē	n.	taxi
叫车	jiàochē		to call for a taxi / car
车钱	chē qián		fare
贵	guì	adj.	expensive
可以	kěyǐ	aux. / adj.	can, may; to be able to
公共汽车	gōnggòng qìchē	n.	bus
地铁	dìtiě	n.	subway
百	bǎi	num.	hundred
便宜	piányi	adj.	cheap

语法点 Language Points

1 “比”字句：用“A 比 B（形容词）”比较性质、程度的差别或高低。例如：

The 比- sentence: the “A 比 B (adjective)” structure is used to compare differences in properties or degree. For example:

他比我高。

He is taller than me.

今天比昨天热。

Today is hotter than yesterday.

坐公共汽车或地铁比坐出租车便宜。

Taking the bus or the subway is cheaper than taking a taxi.

否定词“不”放在“比”的前面，可以构成否定比较句。例如：

The negation word “不” is placed in front of “比” to form a negative comparison sentence. For example:

他不比我高。

He isn't taller than me.

今天不比昨天冷。

Today isn't colder than yesterday.

坐火车不比坐飞机贵。

Taking a train isn't more expensive than taking a plane.

2 助动词“要”：可以表示“需要”的意思。例如：

The auxiliary verb “要”: it means “need to / it is needed” or “it takes”. For example:

从我家到学校要走二十分钟。

It takes me twenty minutes to walk from home to school.

坐出租车去机场要二百块钱。

It costs two hundred yuan to take a taxi to the airport.

他每天要工作八个小时。

He needs to work for eight hours every day.

3 助动词“可以”：表示具备某种客观条件。例如：

The auxiliary verb “可以”: used to indicate a certain objective condition. For example:

一百块钱可以买两件衣服。

One hundred yuan can buy you two articles of clothing.

现在手机上可以叫车了。

Calling for a car can be done on the phone now.

现在天气热了，可以游泳了。

The weather is hot now, it’s appropriate for swimming / we can go swimming.

4 副词“还”：表示除了提到的情况外，另有增补。例如：

The adverb “还”: indicating an auxiliary situation on top of the mentioned one. For example:

你要好好学习，还要好好吃饭。

You have to study hard and you also have to eat well.

这个商店卖水果，还卖衣服。

This store sells fruits and also sells clothes.

手机可以打电话，还可以叫车。

We can use our phones to make phone calls and also to call for cars.

5 “等……再”：表示某一个动作现在还不想或不打算进行，要等做完另一件事以后进行。例如：

“等……再”: indicates an action that we don’t want or don’t plan to do right now, but only do it after another action has been completed. For example:

等车来了再出门。

Leave the house only when the car is here.

等天热了再去游泳。

We'll go swimming when the weather is hot.

等这件衣服便宜了再买。

I'll buy this garment when it's cheaper.

练习 Drills

听力练习 Listening Drills

1 听词语，判断图片是否正确。 06-4

Listen to the words and determine whether the pictures are correct.

_____ _____ _____ _____ _____

2 听句子，选择正确图片。 06-5

Listen to the sentences and choose the correct pictures.

(1)

A

B

C

(2)

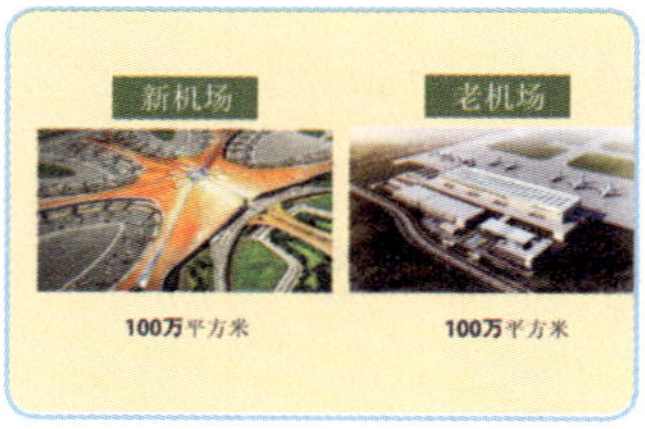

A

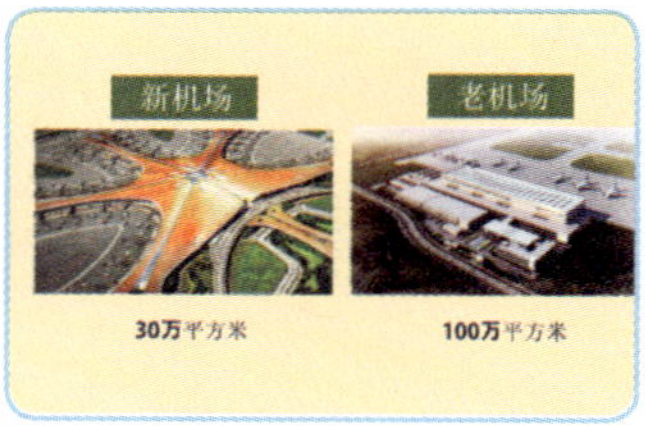

B

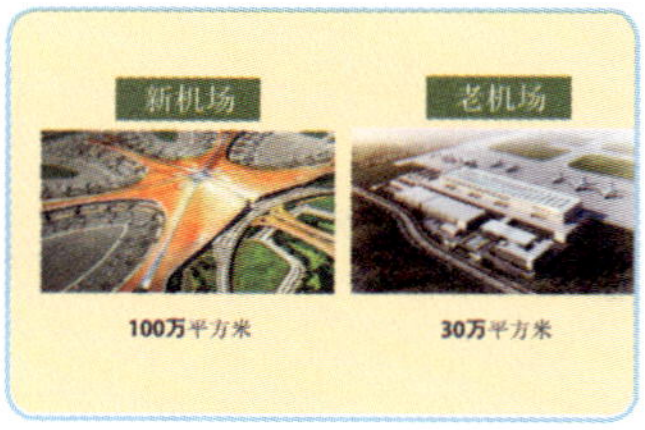

C

（3）

A

B

C

（4）

A

B

C

（5）

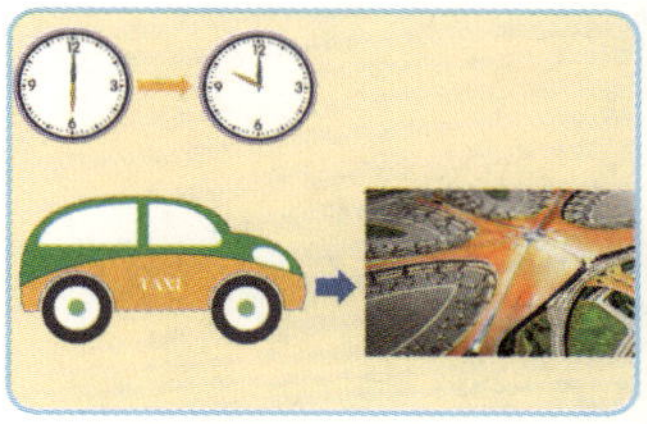
A

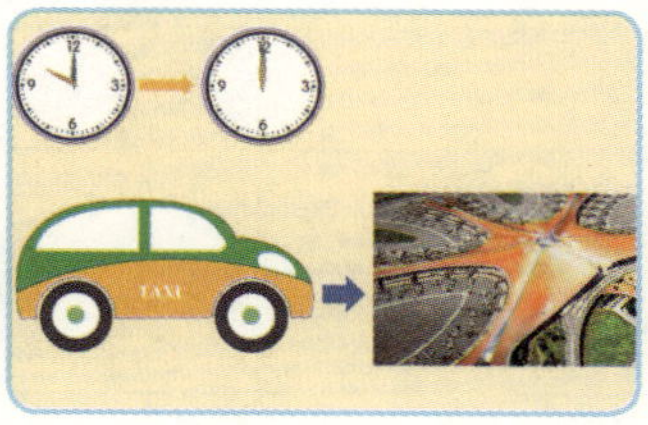
B

C

3 听对话，选择正确图片。 06–6

Listen to the conversations and choose the correct pictures.

A

B

C

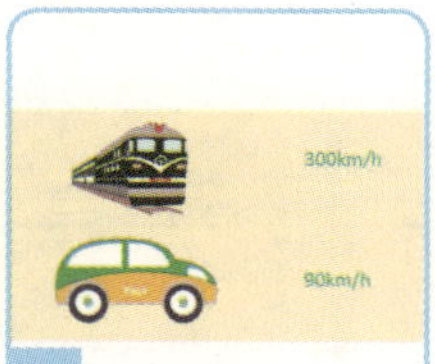

D

E

（1）		（2）	
（3）		（4）	
（5）			

4 听录音，选择正确答案。 06–7

Listen to the recordings and choose the correct answers.

（1）A. 车很少 chē hěn shǎo　B. 车很快 chē hěn kuài　C. 车很大 chē hěn dà　（　　）

（2）A. 很大 hěn dà　B. 很贵 hěn guì　C. 很远 hěn yuǎn　（　　）

	A	B	C	
(3)	yì tiān 一天	yí gè xiǎoshí 一个小时	liǎng gè xiǎoshí 两个小时	(　　)
(4)	dǎ diànhuà 打电话	kàn diànshì 看电视	jiàochē 叫车	(　　)
(5)	èrbǎi kuài qián 二百块钱	yìbǎi kuài qián 一百块钱	èrshí kuài qián 二十块钱	(　　)

口语练习 Speaking Drills

5 听后重复。 06-8

Listen and repeat.

(1) ____________________

(2) ____________________

(3) ____________________

(4) ____________________

(5) ____________________

6 听后回答。 06-9

Listen and answer.

(1) ____________________

(2) ____________________

(3) ____________________

(4) ____________________

(5) ____________________

7 回答问题。

Answer the question.

Shuōshuo zuò gōnggòng qìchē hé dìtiě hǎo bù hǎo .
说说坐公共汽车和地铁好不好。

____

____

7 Lesson Seven

Chá bǐ kāfēi piányi duō le
茶比咖啡便宜多了

Tea is much cheaper than coffee

热身
Warm-up

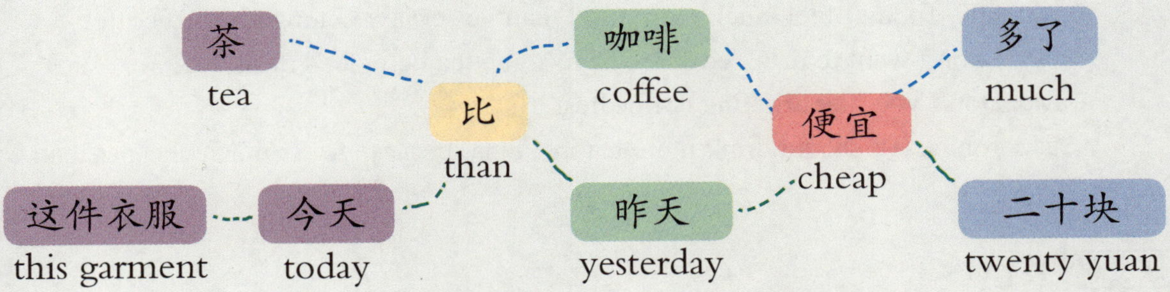

课文 Text

课文 1 07-1

Shālì: Wǒmen yǐjīng xuéxíle yí shàngwǔ le, tài lèi le, xiūxi xiūxi ba.
莎莉：我们已经学习了一上午了，太累了，休息休息吧。

Dàwèi: Hǎo de. Jīntiān bǐ zuótiān lèi duō le. Wǒmen qù hē kāfēi ba.
大卫：好的。今天比昨天累多了。我们去喝咖啡吧。

Shālì: Wǒ bù xiǎng hē kāfēi. Wǒ zhèr yǒu chá, wǒmen hē chá ba.
莎莉：我不想喝咖啡。我这儿有茶，我们喝茶吧。

Dàwèi: Nǐ bú shì zuì xǐhuan hē kāfēi ma?
大卫：你不是最喜欢喝咖啡吗？

Shālì: Wǒ juéde zài Zhōngguó yào duō hē chá, yīnwèi chá bǐ kāfēi piányi duō le.
莎莉：我觉得在中国要多喝茶，因为茶比咖啡便宜多了。

Text One

Sally: We've been studying all morning, I'm so tired, let's take a rest.
David: OK. Today I feel much more tired than yesterday. Let's go have a coffee.
Sally: I don't want to drink coffee. I have some tea here, let's drink tea.
David: Don't you like drinking coffee best?
Sally: I think we should drink more tea in China, because tea is much cheaper than coffee.

课文 2 07-2

Shālì: Zuótiān nǐ bú shì xiǎng gěi Níkè de nǚér mǎi yīfu ma? Mǎile ma?
莎莉：昨天你不是想给尼克的女儿买衣服吗？买了吗？

Dàwèi: Hái méi mǎi ne. Wǒmen xiànzài zài shǒujī shang kànkan ba.
大卫：还没买呢。我们现在在手机上看看吧。

Shālì: Zuótiān nǐ bú shì juéde zhè jiàn yīfu guì ma? Jīntiān piányi le.
莎莉：昨天你不是觉得这件衣服贵吗？今天便宜了。

Dàwèi: Shì de, bǐ zuótiān piányi le èrshí kuài.
大卫：是的，比昨天便宜了二十块。

Shālì: Nǐ zhīdào Níkè de nǚér duō gāo ma?
莎莉：你知道尼克的女儿多高吗？

Dàwèi: Bǐ zhège zhuōzi gāo yìdiǎnr.
大卫：比这个桌子高一点儿。

Text Two

Sally: Weren't you planning on buying clothes for Nick's daughter yesterday? Did you buy any?

David: Not yet. Let's have a look on the phone now.

Sally: Didn't you think this garment was too expensive yesterday? It's cheaper today.

David: Yes, it's twenty yuan cheaper than yesterday.

Sally: Do you know how tall Nick's daughter is?

David: A bit taller than this table.

课文 3 07–3

Jīntiān Shālì hé Dàwèi yìqǐ xuéxíle yí shàngwǔ, zhōngwǔ yìqǐ qù Shālì de fángjiān hē le chá. Shālì bāngzhù Dàwèi zài shǒujī shang gěi Níkè de nǚér mǎile yí jiàn yīfu. Zhè jiàn yīfu jīntiān bǐ zuótiān piányile èrshí kuài qián.

今天莎莉和大卫一起学习了一上午，中午一起去莎莉的房间喝了茶。莎莉帮助大卫在手机上给尼克的女儿买了一件衣服。这件衣服今天比昨天便宜了二十块钱。

Text Three

Sally and David studied together all morning today, at noon they went to Sally's room to drink tea. Sally helped David buy a garment on the phone for Nick's daughter. This garment is twenty yuan cheaper today than it was yesterday.

生词 New Words

休息	xiūxi	v.	to have a rest
还没	hái méi		not yet
件	jiàn	m.	*used with items of clothing*
高	gāo	adj.	tall
一点儿	yìdiǎnr	num.	a bit, a little, some
房间	fángjiān	n.	room
帮助	bāngzhù	v. / n.	to help; help

语法点 Language Points

1 动词重叠：动词重叠后可以表示动作持续的时间短或比较轻松随意的语气。单音节动词重叠后，第二个音节读轻声。双音节动词重叠后，第二和第四个音节读轻声。例如：

Reduplicated verbs: reduplicated verbs can indicate the shortness of an action or a relaxed and casual tone. When reduplicating monosyllabic verbs, the second verb is pronounced in a neutral tone. When reduplicating disyllabic verbs, the second and the fourth syllables are pronounced in a neutral tone. For example:

我可以看看这本书吗？

May I take a look at this book?

我现在每天看看书、喝喝茶，很高兴。

Nowadays I read books and drink tea every day, that makes me very happy.

我们休息休息吧。

Let's take a rest.

2 “比”字句：在“A 比 B（形容词）”句子的形容词后，还可以加上表示具体程度或数量的“一些”“多了”“一点儿”或数量词作补语。例如：

The 比- sentence: in the “A 比 B (adjective)” sentence pattern, the adjective may be followed by words expressing a specific degree or quantity, like “一些” “多了” “一点儿” or numeral-measure words, which form the complement. For example:

茶比咖啡便宜一些。

Tea is a little bit cheaper than coffee.

今天比昨天热多了。

Today is much hotter than yesterday.

尼克的女儿比这个桌子高一点儿。

Nick's daughter is a bit taller than this table.

3 反问句“不是……吗”：一种反问句，基于一个已知的事实或道理，用较弱的反问语气来加以肯定，达到引起注意的目的。例如：

The rhetorical question “不是……吗”: a type of rhetorical question used with the purpose of attracting the attention over an already-known fact or principle by using a slightly soft, rhetorical tone to obtain confirmation. For example:

你不是最喜欢喝咖啡吗？

Don't you like drinking coffee best?

你不是想给尼克的女儿买衣服吗？

Weren't you planning on buying clothes for Nick's daughter?

昨天你不是觉得这件衣服贵吗？

Didn't you think this garment was too expensive yesterday?

4 助动词“要”：表示应该做某事的意思。例如：

The auxiliary verb “要”: indicates that something should be done. For example:

在中国我们要多喝茶。

We should drink more tea in China.

我们要好好学习中文。

We have to study Chinese hard.

明天早上妈妈去机场，我要早点儿起床。

My mom will go to the airport tomorrow morning, so I should get up earlier.

练习 Drills

听力练习 Listening Drills

1 听词语，判断图片是否正确。 07–4

Listen to the words and determine whether the pictures are correct.

(1) ______

(2) ______

(3) ______

(4) ______

(5) ______

2 听句子，选择正确图片。 07–5

Listen to the sentences and choose the correct pictures.

（1）

A

B

C

（2）

A

B

C

（3）

A

B

C

（4）

A

B

C

（5）

A

B

C

3 听对话，选择正确图片。 07–6
Listen to the conversations and choose the correct pictures.

A B C D E

(1)		(2)	
(3)		(4)	
(5)			

4 听录音，选择正确答案。 07–7
Listen to the recordings and choose the correct answers.

(1)	A. 运动 (yùndòng)	B. 休息 (xiūxi)	C. 学习 (xuéxí)	( )
(2)	A. 茶 (chá)	B. 咖啡 (kāfēi)	C. 水 (shuǐ)	( )
(3)	A. 喝茶 (hē chá)	B. 游泳 (yóuyǒng)	C. 跑步 (pǎobù)	( )
(4)	A. 不知道 (bù zhīdào)	B. 贵 (guì)	C. 便宜 (piányi)	( )
(5)	A. 不便宜 (bù piányi)	B. 便宜多了 (piányi duō le)	C. 便宜一点儿 (piányi yìdiǎnr)	( )

口语练习 Speaking Drills

5 听后重复。 07–8
Listen and repeat.

(1) ____________________

(2) ____________________

(3) ____________________

(4) ____________________

(5) ____________________

6 听后回答。 07–9

Listen and answer.

（1）＿＿＿＿＿＿＿＿＿＿＿＿

（2）＿＿＿＿＿＿＿＿＿＿＿＿

（3）＿＿＿＿＿＿＿＿＿＿＿＿

（4）＿＿＿＿＿＿＿＿＿＿＿＿

（5）＿＿＿＿＿＿＿＿＿＿＿＿

7 回答问题。

Answer the question.

Shuōshuo nǐ zhīdào de Zhōngguó chá .
说说 你知道的 中国 茶。

8 Lesson Eight

Wǒ hái méi qùguo nàr

我还没去过那儿

I haven't been there yet

热身 Warm-up

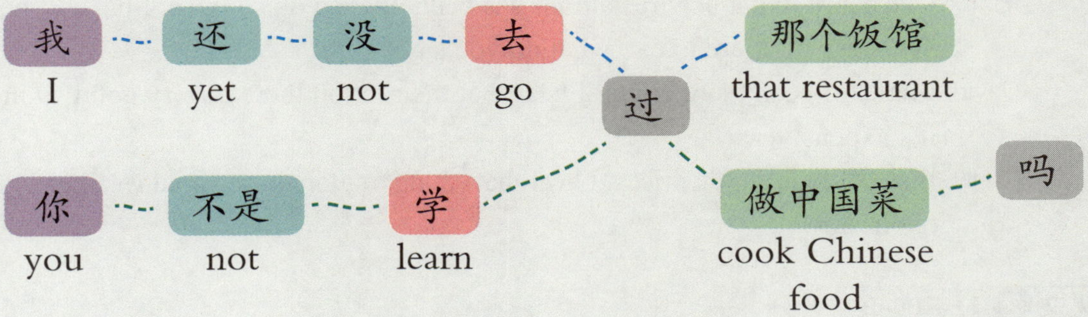

课文 Text

课文 1 08-1

Dàwèi: Zhōngwǔ nǐ xiǎng chī shénme?
大卫：中午 你想吃什么？

Shālì: Tīngshuō xuéxiào li xīn kāile yì jiā fànguǎnr. Wǒ hái méi qùguo nàr. Wǒmen qù nàr chī, zěnmeyàng?
莎莉：听说 学校里新开了一家饭馆儿。我还没去过那儿。我们去那儿吃，怎么样？

Dàwèi: Wǒ yě méi qùguo. Wǒ tīngshuō nàr de yángròu hěn hǎochī. Bù zhīdào guì bú guì.
大卫：我也没去过。我听说那儿的羊肉很好吃。不知道贵不贵。

Shālì: Guì yìdiǎnr méi guānxi, wǒ tīngshuō tiānqì lěng de shíhou, chī yángròu duì shēntǐ hǎo.
莎莉：贵一点儿没关系，我听说天气冷的时候，吃羊肉对身体好。

Text One

David: What do you want to eat at lunch?

Sally: I've heard that a new restaurant has been opened on campus. I haven't been there yet. Let's go there to eat, what do you say?

David: I haven't been there either. I hear that the mutton there is very good. Don't know if it's expensive.

Sally: It's OK if it's a little pricey, I hear that eating mutton during cold weather is good for our health.

课文 2 08-2

Shālì: Nǐ bú shì xuéguo zuò Zhōngguó cài ma? Xué huìle jǐ gè cài?
莎莉：你不是学过做中国菜吗？学会了几个菜？

Dàwèi: Wǒ xuéguo jǐ tiān, dànshì méi xuéhuì jǐ gè cài.
大卫：我学过几天，但是没学会几个菜。

Shālì : Nǐ xuéhuìle shénme?
莎莉：你学会了什么？

Dàwèi : Wǒ xuéhuìle zuò jīdàn miàn.
大卫：我学会了做鸡蛋面。

Text Two

Sally: Haven't you learned to cook Chinese food? How many dishes did you learn how to make?
David: I learned for a few days, but didn't really master many dishes.
Sally: What did you learn how to make?
David: I learned how to make egg noodles.

课文 3 08–3

Xuéxiào li xīn kāile yì jiā fànguǎnr, Dàwèi hé Shālì dōu méi qùguo nàr. Tīngshuō nàli yángròu zuò de hěn hǎochī. Shālì xiǎng qù nàr chī yángròu, yīnwèi tā tīngshuō tiānqì lěng de shíhou, chī yángròu duì shēntǐ hǎo.
学校里新开了一家饭馆儿，大卫和莎莉都没去过那儿。听说那里羊肉做得很好吃。莎莉想去那儿吃羊肉，因为她听说天气冷的时候，吃羊肉对身体好。

Text Three

A new restaurant was newly opened on campus, neither David nor Sally have been there yet. They've heard that they make a very tasty mutton there. Sally wants to go there to eat mutton, because she's heard that eating mutton in cold weather is good for our health.

生词 New Words

家	jiā	m.	*used with companies, restaurants, shops, etc.*
过	guo	part.	*used ofter a verb to indicate a past action or state*
学会	xuéhuì	v.	to learn, to master
做（菜）	zuò (cài)	v.	to cook
鸡蛋面	jīdàn miàn		egg noodles

语法点 Language Points

1 动态助词“过”：“过”放在动词后，表示有过某种经历。肯定形式是“verb + 过”，否定形式是“没 + verb + 过”。例如：

The aspectual particle “过”: “过” is placed after the verb to indicate that something has happened. The affirmative form is “verb + 过”, whereas the negative form is “没 + verb + 过”. For example:

我去过那个饭馆。

I’ve been to that restaurant.

我学过做中国菜。

I’ve learned how to cook Chinese food.

他没去过北京。

He hasn’t been to Beijing.

2 动词“听说”：用“听说”时，不强调消息的来源及其可靠性。可以有主语，也可以没有。例如：

The verb “听说”: when we use “听说”, we’re not emphasizing the source of the information or its reliability. It can come with a subject or without one. For example:

（我）听说学校里新开了一个饭馆。

I’ve heard a new restaurant was opened on campus.

（我）听说那个饭馆的菜很好吃。

They say that restaurant serves very good food.

（我）听说尼克生病了。

I’ve heard that Nick is sick.

3 结果补语：表示动作或状态的结果。当叙述一个动作引起某个具体结果时，就应该用结果补语。例如：

The complement of result: it expresses the result of an action or a state. We should use the complement of result when a specific result is derived from the action that is being recounted. For example:

你学会了几个菜？

How many dishes did you learn how to make?

我买到了一张电影票。

I bought a cinema ticket.

我听懂了老师的意思。

I understood what the teacher meant.

4 “几个”：这里的“几个”不是表示疑问的，是疑问代词的虚指用法。“几个”可以和“没”搭配表示数量少。例如：

“几个”: this is not the common usage of “几个” of asking a question, but rather an empty usage of the interrogative pronoun, which is used together with “没” to indicate a small quantity or amount. For example:

他们几个喝茶，我们几个喝咖啡。

They're drinking tea, we're drinking coffee.

我没看见几个人。

I saw only a few people.

今天学校里没几个人。

There's only a handful of people at school today.

练习 Drills

听力练习 Listening Drills

1 听词语，判断图片是否正确。08-4

Listen to the words and determine whether the pictures are correct.

(1) ____

(2) ____

(3) ____

(4) ____

(5) ____

2 听句子，选择正确图片。 08–5
Listen to the sentences and choose the correct pictures.

（1）

A

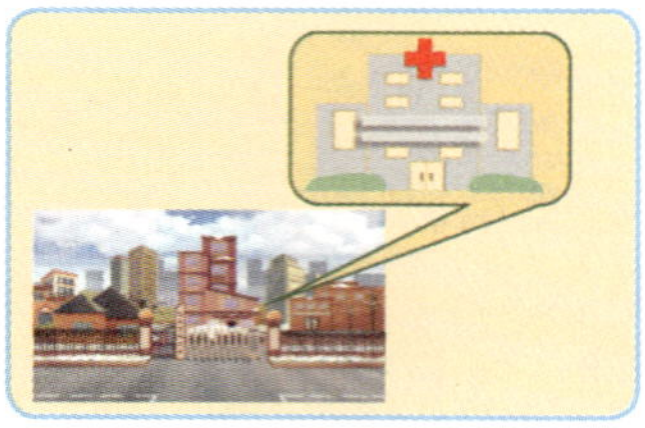
B

C

（2）

A

B

C

（3）

A

B

C

（4）

A

B

C

（5）

A

B

C

3 听对话，选择正确图片。 08–6

Listen to the conversations and choose the correct pictures.

A

B

C

D

E

(1)		(2)	
(3)		(4)	
(5)			

4 听录音，选择正确答案。 08–7

Listen to the recordings and choose the correct answers.

	A	B	C	
(1)	A. fànguǎn 饭馆	B. shāngdiàn 商店	C. jiàoshì 教室	(　)
(2)	A. qùguo 去过	B. méi qùguo 没去过	C. bù zhīdào 不知道	(　)
(3)	A. tiānqì rè de shíhou 天气热的时候	B. xià yǔ de shíhou 下雨的时候	C. tiānqì lěng de shíhou 天气冷的时候	(　)
(4)	A. méi xuéguo 没学过	B. xuéguo 学过	C. méi xuéhuì 没学会	(　)
(5)	A. bù duō 不多	B. hěn duō 很多	C. méiyǒu 没有	(　)

口语练习 Speaking Drills

5 听后重复。 08–8

Listen and repeat.

(1) ____________________

(2) ____________________

(3) ____________________

(4) ____________________

(5) ____________________

6 听后回答。 08–9

Listen and answer.

(1) ______________________________

(2) ______________________________

(3) ______________________________

(4) ______________________________

(5) ______________________________

7 回答问题。

Answer the question.

Shuōshuo nǐ zhīdào de Zhōngguó cài .
说说 你 知道 的 中国 菜。

____

____

9 Lesson Nine

Wǒ gěi nín wèn yíxià

我给您问一下

I'll go ask about it

热身 Warm-up

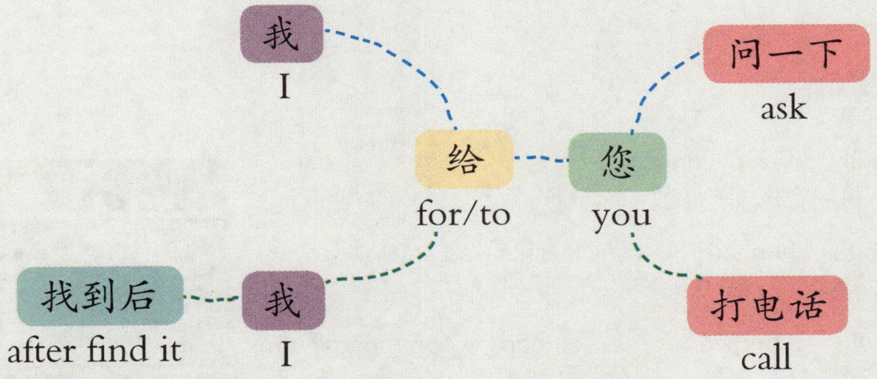

课文 Text

课文1 09-1

Shālì: Duìbuqǐ, ràng wǒ kàn yíxià nín de yǐzi hòumiàn, hǎoma?
莎莉：对不起，让我看一下您的椅子后面，好吗？

Gùkè: Zěnme le? Nǐ zài zhǎo shénme?
顾客：怎么了？你在找什么？

Shālì: Wǒ zài zhǎo shǒujī, nín yǒu méi yǒu kàndào yí gè hóngsè de shǒujī?
莎莉：我在找手机，您有没有看到一个红色的手机？

Gùkè: Méi kàndào, nǐ wèn yíxià fúwùyuán ba.
顾客：没看到，你问一下服务员吧。

Text One

Sally: Excuse me, let me have a look behind your chair, OK?
Customer: What's wrong? What are you looking for?
Sally: I'm looking for my mobile phone, have you seen a red mobile phone?
Customer: I haven't seen it, go ask the waiter.

课文2 09-2

Shālì: Fúwùyuán, nǐ hǎo.
莎莉：服务员，你好。

Fúwùyuán: Nínhǎo! Nín yǒu shìr ma?
服务员：您好！您有事儿吗？

Shālì: Qǐngwèn, nǐ kàndào yí gè hóngsè de shǒujī le ma?
莎莉：请问，你看到一个红色的手机了吗？

Fúwùyuán: Wǒ méi kàndào. Wǒ gěi nín wèn yíxià. Nín gěi wǒ yí gè diànhuà hàomǎ, zhǎodào hòu wǒ gěi nín dǎ diànhuà. Nín zuò de shì jǐ hào zhuōzi?
服务员：我没看到。我给您问一下。您给我一个电话号码，找到后我给您打电话。您坐的是几号桌子？

Shālì: Wǒ zuò de shì èr hào zhuō.
莎莉：我坐的是二号桌。

Text Two

Sally: Hello!
Waitress: Hello! How can I help?
Sally: I'm sorry, have you seen a red mobile phone?
Waitress: I haven't seen it. I'll go ask about it. Could you please give me a cellphone number? And I'll call you after we find it. What table were you sitting at?
Sally: I was sitting at table number two.

课文 3 09-3

Shālì de shǒujī bú jiàn le . Tā zhōngwǔ shì
莎莉的手机不见了。她中午是
zài fànguǎn chī de fàn . Xiàwǔ tā qù fànguǎn zhǎo
在饭馆吃的饭。下午她去饭馆找
shǒujī, dàjiā dōu méi kàndào . Fúwùyuán shuō ,
手机，大家都没看到。服务员说，
zhǎodào hòu gěi tā dǎ diànhuà . Wǎnshang , fúwùyuán gěi tā dǎ diànhuà shuō , shǒujī
找到后给她打电话。晚上，服务员给她打电话说，手机
zài sān hào zhuō xiàmiàn .
在三号桌下面。

Text Three

Sally couldn't find her mobile phone. She had lunch at the restaurant at noon. She went to the restaurant in the afternoon to look for her phone, but nobody had seen it. The waitress told her that they would call her after they found the phone. In the evening, the waitress called her and said the phone was under table number three.

生词 New Words

让	ràng	v.	to let
找	zhǎo	v.	to look for, to try to find
看（到）	kàn (dào)	v.	to see
红色	hóngsè	adj.	red
服务员	fúwùyuán	n.	attendant, waiter / waitress

续表

有事儿	yǒushìr		to have sth. on one's mind; to be preoccupied (*here used to asked what the matter is*)
电话号码	diànhuà hàomǎ		telephone number
后	hòu	n.	after
下面	xiàmiàn	n.	under

语法点 Language Points

1 "让"：句子的第一个动词是"让"等表示使令意思的词时，句子的宾语兼作后面补语短语（或补语从句）的主语，这样的句子叫作兼语句。例如：

"让": when the first verb of the sentence is "让" or other words expressing a command, the object of that sentence also serves as the subject of the succeeding sentence. This type of sentence is called a pivotal sentence. For example:

让我看一下您的椅子后面，好吗？

Let me have a look behind your chair, OK?

妈妈让我多运动。

My mom has asked me to exercise often.

妈妈不让女儿去机场。

The mother doesn't allow her daughter to go to the airport.

2 用"好吗"的是非问句：说话人先提出自己的意见，然后征询对方意见，这时就可以用"好吗"。例如：

Yes-no questions with "好吗": the speaker presents their suggestion first and then asks for the listener's opinion by using "好吗". For example:

让我看一下你的椅子后面，好吗？

Let me have a look behind your chair, OK?

我们明天一起去跑步，好吗？

Let's go running together tomorrow, what do you say?

我们中午一起去商店买东西，好吗？

Let's go together to the store at noon to buy stuff, all right?

3 “是……的”：当“是……的”中间的动词带宾语时，“的”可以在动词之后、宾语之前。例如：

The structure “是……的”: when the verb within the “是……的” structure takes an object, “的” may be placed after the verb, just before the object. For example:

她中午是在饭馆吃的饭。

She had lunch at the restaurant at noon.

我是在北京学的中文。

I learned Chinese in Beijing.

昨天他是六点回的家。

He came back home at 6 o'clock yesterday.

4 时间名词“后”：表示某个时间或某个动作以后的时间。例如：

The time noun “后”: it indicates a time that follows a specific time or action. For example:

七点后给我打电话吧。

Call me after seven.

我一个小时后回来。

I'll come back after one hour.

找到手机后我给您打电话。

I'll call you after we find your phone.

练习 Drills

听力练习 Listening Drills

1 听词语，判断图片是否正确。 09-4

Listen to the words and determine whether the pictures are correct.

(1) ______

(2) ______

(3) ______

(4) ______

(5) ______

2 听句子，选择正确图片。 09–5

Listen to the sentences and choose the correct pictures.

（1）

A

B

C

（2）

A

B

C

（3）

A

B

C

（4）

A

B

C

（5）

A

B

C

3 听对话，选择正确图片。 09-6

Listen to the conversations and choose the correct pictures.

A

B

C

D

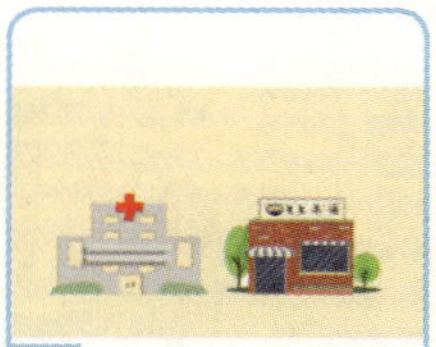
E

(1)		(2)	
(3)		(4)	
(5)			

4 听录音，选择正确答案。 09-7

Listen to the recordings and choose the correct answers.

(1)	A. wǒ de 我的	B. péngyou de 朋友的	C. tóngxué de 同学的	(　　)
(2)	A. shǒujī 手机	B. hóngsè 红色	C. zhuōzi 桌子	(　　)
(3)	A. jiā li 家里	B. xuéxiào 学校	C. fànguǎn 饭馆	(　　)
(4)	A. fúwùyuán 服务员	B. wǒ 我	C. péngyou 朋友	(　　)
(5)	A. zǎoshang 早上	B. xiàwǔ 下午	C. wǎnshang 晚上	(　　)

口语练习 Speaking Drills

5 听后重复。 09-8

Listen and repeat.

(1) ______

(2) ______

(3) ______

(4) ______

(5) ______

6 听后回答。 09-9

Listen and answer.

(1) ____________________

(2) ____________________

(3) ____________________

(4) ____________________

(5) ____________________

7 选词填空，读一读。

Fill in the blanks with the words and then read the text.

A. 后 (hòu)　B. 是 (shì)　C. 都 (dōu)　D. 给 (gěi)　E. 不 (bú)

Shālì de shǒujī jiàn le. Tā zhōngwǔ zài fànguǎn chī de fàn. Xiàwǔ tā qù fànguǎn zhǎo shǒujī, dàjiā méi kàndào, fúwùyuán shuō, zhǎodào gěi tā dǎ diànhuà. Wǎnshang, fúwùyuán tā dǎ diànhuà shuō, shǒujī zài sān hào zhuō xiàmiàn.

莎莉的手机（　）见了。她中午（　）在饭馆吃的饭。下午她去饭馆找手机，大家（　）没看到，服务员说，找到（　）给她打电话。晚上，服务员（　）她打电话说，手机在三号桌下面。

Lesson Ten

10 走路十几分钟就到了

Zǒulù shíjǐ fēnzhōng jiù dào le

Walking here takes just a little over ten minutes

热身 Warm-up

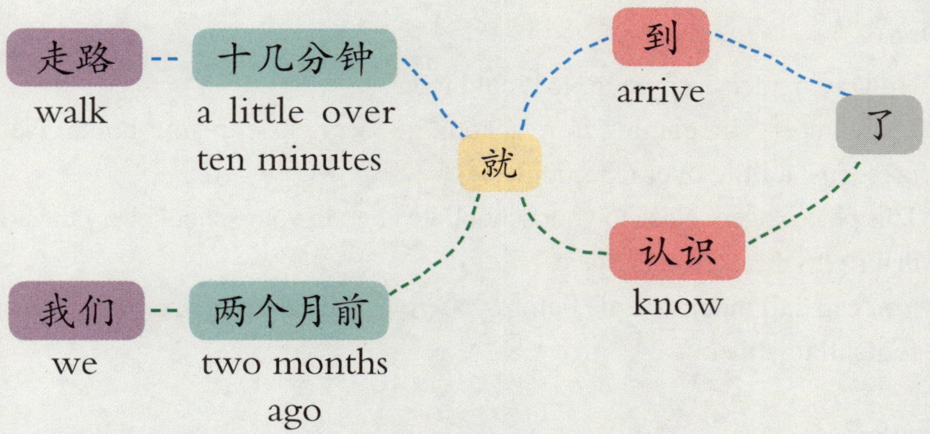

课文 Text

课文 1 10–1

Níkè: Dàwèi, nǐ hǎo, qǐng jìn. Jīntiān lěng bù lěng?
尼克：大卫，你好，请进。今天冷不冷？

Dàwèi: Bù lěng. Wǒ cóng xuéxiào lái, xuéxiào lí nǐ jiā hěn jìn. Zǒulù shíjǐ fēnzhōng jiù dào le.
大卫：不冷。我从学校来，学校离你家很近。走路十几分钟就到了。

Níkè: Yīnwèi zhèr lí nǐmen xuéxiào hěn jìn, wǒ kěyǐ tiāntiān qù nǐmen xuéxiào yùndòng, suǒyǐ wǒ zūle zhèlǐ.
尼克：因为这儿离你们学校很近，我可以天天去你们学校运动，所以我租了这里。

Dàwèi: Xià cì nǐ qù xuéxiào yùndòng qián kěyǐ gàosu wǒ, wǒmen kěyǐ yìqǐ tī zúqiú.
大卫：下次你去学校运动前可以告诉我，我们可以一起踢足球。

Text One

Nick: Hi, David, please come in. Is it cold today?

David: It's not cold. I'm coming from school, it's very close to your home. Walking here takes just a little over ten minutes.

Nick: This place is very close to your school, I can go to your school every day to exercise, that's why I rented this place.

David: You can call me next time before you go to the school to exercise, we can play football together.

课文 2 10–2

Níkè: Dàwèi, wǒ lái jièshào yíxià, zhè shì wǒ de qīzi.
尼克：大卫，我来介绍一下，这是我的妻子。

Níkè qīzi: Hěn gāoxìng rènshi nǐ. Wǒ tīng
尼克妻子：很高兴认识你。我听

Níkè shuōguo, nǐmen liǎng gè duō yuè qián jiù rènshi le.
尼克说过，你们两个多月前就认识了。

Dàwèi: Shì de, shíjiān guò de zhēn kuài, nà tiān wǒ qù yīyuàn, Níkè yě qù yīyuàn kāiyào. Wǒ láiguo nín jiā yí cì, nín bú zài jiā.
大卫：是的，时间过得真快，那天我去医院，尼克也去医院开药。我来过您家一次，您不在家。

Níkè qīzi: Shì de, nà tiān wǒ yǒu gōngzuò.
尼克妻子：是的，那天我有工作。

Text Two

Nick: David, let me introduce you to my wife.

Nick's wife: Nice to meet you. I've heard Nick saying that you two met two months ago.

David: That's right. Time flies. That day I was at the hospital, Nick was there too for a prescription. I've been to your house once before, but you weren't home.

Nick's wife: Right, I was working that day.

课文 3 10–3

Jīntiān shì Níkè nǚ'ér de shēngrì. Dàwèi gěi tā mǎile yí jiàn piàoliang de yīfu, zhù tā shēngrì kuàilè. Zài Níkè jiā, Dàwèi dì-yī cì jiàndàole Níkè de qīzi. Níkè de qīzi zuò cài zuò de hěn hǎo. Tā zuòle hěn duō hǎochī de cài, dàjiā yìqǐ chī de hěn gāoxìng.
今天是尼克女儿的生日。大卫给她买了一件漂亮的衣服，祝她生日快乐。在尼克家，大卫第一次见到了尼克的妻子。尼克的妻子做菜做得很好。她做了很多好吃的菜，大家一起吃得很高兴。

Text Three

Today was Nick's daughter's birthday. David bought her a beautiful garment to wish her a happy birthday. At Nick's house, David saw Nick's wife for the first time. Nick's wife cooks very well. She made many delicious dishes, and they all ate happily together.

生词 New Words

进	jìn	v.	to go in
离	lí	v.	to be away from, to be at a distance from
近	jìn	adj.	close
走路	zǒulù	v.	to walk
所以	suǒyǐ	conj.	so, therefore
租	zū	v.	to rent
前	qián	n.	front, in front
妻子	qīzi	n.	wife
开（药）	kāi (yào)	v.	to prescribe medicine
那天	nà tiān		that day
生日	shēngrì	n.	birthday
祝	zhù	v.	to wish
快乐	kuàilè	adj.	happy
见到	jiàndào		to see

语法点 Language Points

1 动词“离”：表示两个地方或物体之间存在距离。例如：

The verb “离”: it indicates that a distance exists between two places or objects. For example:

我们学校离你家很近。

Our school is very close to your home.

我家离机场不远。

My house isn't far from the airport.

你的眼睛离电脑太近了。

Your eyes are too close to the computer.

2 时间名词“前”：表示某个时间或某个动作以前的时间。例如：

The time noun “前”: it indicates a time prior to a specific time or action. For example:

七点前给我打电话。
Call me before seven o'clock.
我是一个小时前回来的。
I came back one hour ago.
吃饭前要洗手。
We have to wash our hands before eating.

3 副词"就"：用在表示时间的词语后，表示说话人认为动作发生得早、快或用的时间少。"就"在句中轻读，句尾经常用"了"。例如：

The adverb "就": it is used after words which indicate time to express the speaker's belief that the action took place early, quickly or that little time was needed. "就" is pronounced in a neutral tone and is commonly accompanied by "了" at the end of the sentence. For example:

走路十几分钟就到了。
Walking here takes just a little over ten minutes.
我们两个月前就认识了。
We met more than two months ago.
他去年就开始学习中文了。
He started learning Chinese last year.

4 "听……说过"：在需要说明信息来源的时候，可以在"听说"中间插入信息来源人，同时用"过"表示曾经发生。例如：

"听……说过": when we need to indicate the source of the information, we can insert the person who is this source within "听说" and also use "过" to indicate that it has already taken place. For example:

听尼克说过，你们两个月前就认识了。
I've heard Nick saying that you two met two months ago.
我听妈妈说过，北京很好。
I've heard my mom saying that Beijing is very nice.
大卫听莎莉说过，跑步对身体很好。
David heard Sally saying that running is good for our health.

5 动量补语"一次"：在句中作动量补语，当动量补语与表示确定的人、物或地点的宾语同时出现时，可以宾语在前，也可以补语在前。例如：

The complement of frequency "一次": it acts as a complement of frequency. When both a complement of frequency and an object indicating a certain person, thing or place are present in a sentence at the same time, the object may be placed either before or after the complement. For example:

我来过您家一次。= 我来过一次您家。

I've been to your house once. = I've been once to your house.

我去过北京一次。= 我去过一次北京。

I've been in Beijing once. = I've been once in Beijing.

我找过老师两次。= 我找过两次老师。

I've looked for the teacher twice. = I've looked twice for the teacher.

练习 Drills

听力练习 Listening Drills

1 听词语，判断图片是否正确。 10–4

Listen to the words and determine whether the pictures are correct.

(1) ______

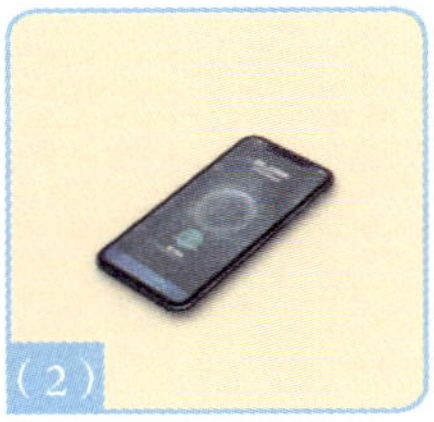
(2) ______

(3) ______

(4) ______

(5) ______

2 听句子，选择正确图片。 10–5

Listen to the sentences and choose the correct pictures.

(1)

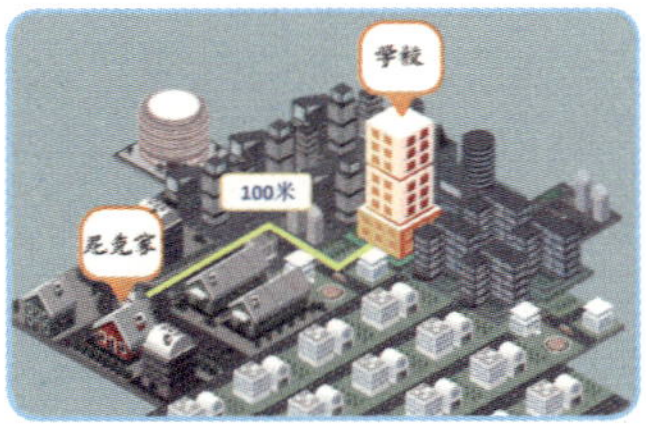

A

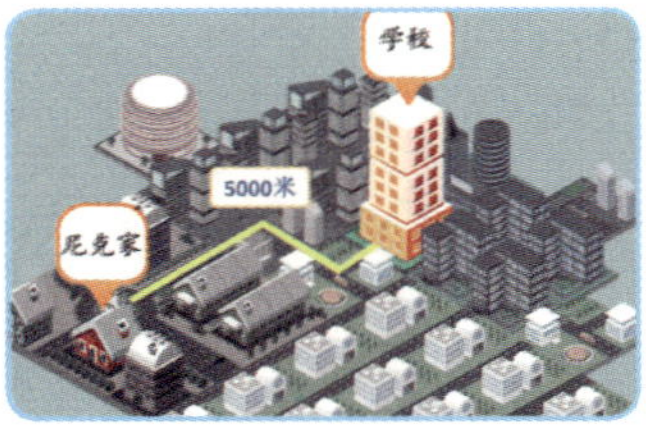

B

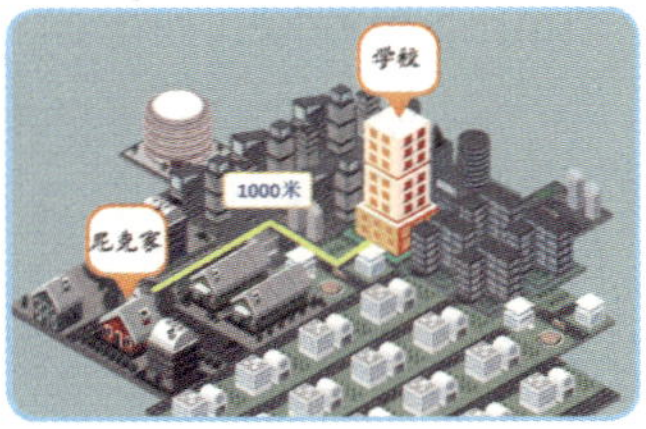

C

(2)

A

B

C

（3）

A

B

C

（4）

A

B

C

（5）

A

B

C

3 听对话，选择正确图片。 10–6
Listen to the conversations and choose the correct pictures.

A

B

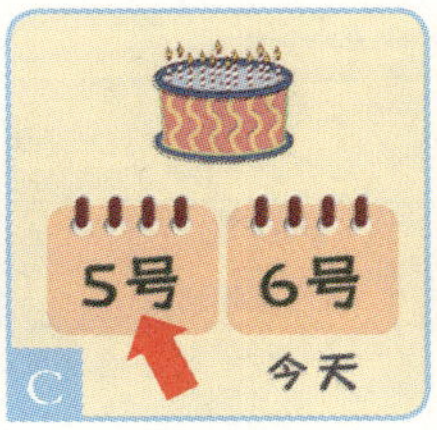

C

D

E

（1）		（2）	
（3）		（4）	
（5）			

4 听录音，选择正确答案。 10–7
Listen to the recordings and choose the correct answers.

（1）A. 很近 (hěn jìn)　　B. 很远 (hěn yuǎn)　　C. 很快 (hěn kuài)　　（　　）

(2) A. wǔ fēnzhōng 五分钟	B. shí fēnzhōng 十分钟	C. sì fēnzhōng 四分钟	( )
(3) A. Níkè 尼克	B. Níkè qīzi 尼克妻子	C. Níkè nǚér 尼克女儿	( )
(4) A. wǒ de 我的	B. háizi de 孩子的	C. wǒ nǚér de 我女儿的	( )
(5) A. yí cì 一次	B. méi lái guo 没来过	C. liǎng cì 两次	( )

口语练习 Speaking Drills

5 听后重复。 10–8
Listen and repeat.

(1) ______

(2) ______

(3) ______

(4) ______

(5) ______

6 听后回答。 10–9
Listen and answer.

(1) ______

(2) ______

(3) ______

(4) ______

(5) ______

7 回答问题。
Answer the question.

Qǐng jièshào yíxià nǐ de yí gè péngyou hé tā de jiārén .
请介绍一下你的一个朋友和他的家人。

______

______

11 Lesson Eleven

Lǎoshī ràng nǐ zài mén wài děngzhe

老师让你在门外等着

The teacher asked you to wait outside the door

热身 Warm-up

老师	让	你	在门外	等	着
teacher	let	you	outside the door	wait	

课文 Text

课文 1 11–1

Wáng lǎoshī : Dàwèi, nǐ hǎo, qǐng zuò.
王 老师：大卫，你好，请 坐。

Nǐ zhǔnbèi de shì nǎ gè wèntí ?
你 准备 的是哪个问题？

Dàwèi : Wǒ zhǔnbèi de shì dì-yī gè wèntí.
大卫：我 准备 的是第一个问题。

Wáng lǎoshī : Wǒmen xiànzài kāishǐ kǎoshì, shíjiān shì sān fēnzhōng.
王 老师：我们 现在 开始 考试，时间 是 三 分钟 。

Dàwèi : Wǒ de jiā zài Yīngguó, fángzi suīrán bù tài dà, dànshì hěn xīn. Fángzi qiánmiàn shì lù, hòumiàn yě shì lù, xiàng zuǒbian zǒu wǔ fēnzhōng yǒu fànguǎnr, xiàng yòubian zǒu shí fēnzhōng yǒu shāngdiàn, pángbiān bù yuǎn háiyǒu xuéxiào. Fángzi li yǒu sì gè shuìjiào de fángjiān. Měi gè fángjiān dōu yǒu zhuōzi, yǐzi, diànnǎo hé diànshì. Wǒ měi tiān wǎnshang dōu yòng diànnǎo xuéxí zhōngwén, suǒyǐ diànnǎo měi tiān dōu shì kāizhe de.
大卫：我的家在 英国，房子 虽然 不太大，但是 很 新。房子 前面 是路，后面 也是路，向 左边 走 五 分钟 有 饭馆儿，向 右边 走 十 分钟 有 商店 ，旁边 不 远 还有 学校。房子里有四个 睡觉 的 房间 。每个 房间 都 有 桌子、椅子、电脑 和 电视。我 每天 晚上 都 用 电脑 学习 中文 ，所以 电脑 每天 都是 开着 的。

Wáng lǎoshī : Hǎo de, nǐ de kǎoshì wán le. Qǐng nǐ jiào yíxià Shālì, ràng tā zài mén wài děngzhe.
王 老师：好 的，你的 考试 完 了。请 你 叫一下 莎莉，让 她 在 门 外 等着 。

Text One

Teacher Wang: Hello, David, please have a seat. Which question did you prepare?

David: I prepared the first question.

Teacher Wang: We'll begin the exam now, the duration is three minutes.

David: My home is in the UK, although the house is not very big, it's rather new. There's a road in front of the house as well as one behind the house. There are restaurants five minutes on foot towards the left, shops ten minutes on foot towards the right, and there's also a school nearby. There are four bedrooms in the house. There are tables, chairs, computers and TV sets in each room. I use my computer every evening to learn Chinese, so my computer is on every day.

Teacher Wang: All right, your exam is over. Please call Sally and ask her to wait outside the door.

课文 2 11-2

Dàwèi: Shālì, lǎoshī ràng nǐ zài mén wài děngzhe.
大卫：莎莉，老师让你在门外等着。

Shālì: Nǐ kǎoshì de shíjiān zhēn cháng!
莎莉：你考试的时间真长！

Lǎoshī wènle nǐ jǐ gè wèntí?
老师问了你几个问题？

Dàwèi: Lǎoshī wènle wǒ liǎng gè wèntí, wǒ juéde wǒ huídá de hěn kuài.
大卫：老师问了我两个问题，我觉得我回答得很快。

Shālì: Kǎoshì de rén juéde shíjiān hěn kuài, dànshì děngzhe de rén juéde shíjiān hěn màn.
莎莉：考试的人觉得时间很快，但是等着的人觉得时间很慢。

Text Two

David: Sally, the teacher asked you to wait outside the door.

Sally: You were in the exam for a really long time! How many questions did the teacher ask you?

David: The teacher asked me two questions, I feel I answered very quickly.

Sally: Those taking the exam feel it's very fast, but those waiting feel it's very slow.

课文 3 11-3

Jīntiān wǒmen kǎoshì. Wǒ zhǔnbèi de wèntí shì jièshào wǒ de jiā. Lǎoshī tīngle wǒ de jièshào hòu, wènle wǒ liǎng gè wèntí. Wǒ juéde wǒ huídá de hěn kuài, dànshì Shālì zài wàimiàn děngzhe, tā juéde wǒ kǎoshì de shíjiān hěn cháng.

今天我们考试。我准备的问题是介绍我的家。老师听了我的介绍后，问了我两个问题。我觉得我回答得很快，但是莎莉在外面等着，她觉得我考试的时间很长。

Text Three

Today we had an exam. The question I prepared was about introducing my home. After listening to my introduction, the teacher asked me two questions. I feel I answered very quickly, but Sally who was waiting outside thought my exam took a long time.

生词 New Words

准备	zhǔnbèi	v.	to prepare
问题	wèntí	n.	question
考试	kǎoshì	n.	test, exam
房子	fángzi	n.	house
虽然	suīrán	conj.	although
路	lù	n.	road
左边	zuǒbian	n.	left side
右边	yòubian	n.	right side
旁边	pángbiān	n.	beside
用	yòng	v.	to use
开	kāi	v.	to turn on
着	zhe	part.	*used after a verb or an adjective to indicate the continuation of an action or state*
完	wán	v.	to finish
外（面）	wài (miàn)	n.	outside
回答	huídá	v.	to answer
慢	màn	adj.	slow

语法点 Language Points

1 “虽然……但是……”：是表示转折关系的关联词，把两个在意义上有转折关系的句子组合在一起，构成转折关系的复句。“虽然”分句在前时，可以省略“虽然”。例如：

“虽然……但是……”: these are connectors indicating a transition; they bring together two sentences that have a relationship of transition, turning them into transitional clauses. If the clause containing “虽然” is in the front, the word “虽然” may be omitted. For example:

虽然房子不大，但是很新。

Although the house isn't very big, it's very new.

虽然我的房间是最小的，但是我觉得是最漂亮的。

Although my room is the smallest one, I think it's the most beautiful one.

这儿的苹果很便宜，但是买的人不多。

These apples are cheap, but not many people are buying them.

2 "不太 + 形容词"：跟"不 + 形容词比"，"不太"减弱了否定的语气，降低了否定的程度。例如：

"不太 + adjective": compared to "不 + adjective", "不太" weakens the tone of the negation or diminishes the degree of the negation. For example:

今天不太累。

I'm not very tired today.

这件衣服不太贵。

This garment isn't too expensive.

这次考试的时间不太长。

This exam didn't take that long.

3 "向 + 方向 + 动词"：表示面向某个方向行动。例如：

"向 + direction + verb": indicates moving towards a certain direction. For example:

A: 去火车站怎么走？

A: How can I get to the railway station?

B: 向东走。

B: Go (towards) east.

请向前看。

Please look ahead.

不要向左边走，向右边走。

Don't walk to the left, walk to the right.

4 动态助词"着"：表示动作或状态的持续。例如：

The aspectual particle "着": it expresses the continuity of an action or state. For example:

他在路上慢慢地走着。

He is walking slowly on the road.

他在教室里坐着。

He is sitting in the classroom.

老师让你在门外等着。

The teacher asked you to wait outside the door.

练习 Drills

听力练习 Listening Drills

1 听词语，判断图片是否正确。 11-4
Listen to the words and determine whether the pictures are correct.

（1）

（2）

（3）

（4）

（5）

2 听句子，选择正确图片。 11-5
Listen to the sentences and choose the correct pictures.

（1）

A

B

C

（2）

A

B

C

（3）

A

B

C

(4)

A

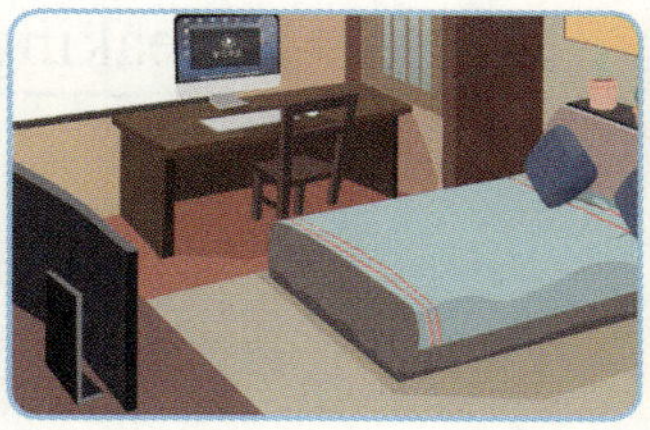
B

C

(5)

A

B

C

3 听对话，选择正确图片。 11-6
Listen to the conversations and choose the correct pictures.

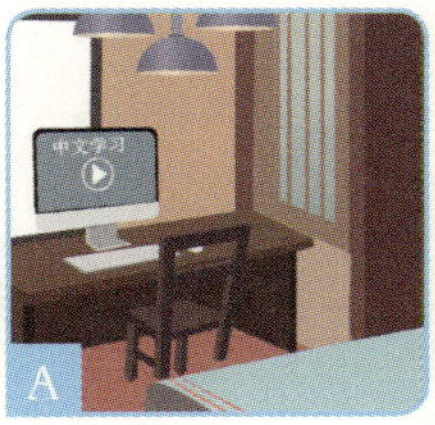
A

B

C

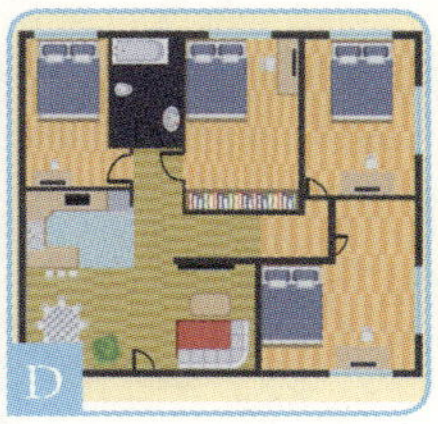
D

E

(1)		(2)	
(3)		(4)	
(5)			

4 听录音，选择正确答案。 11-7
Listen to the recordings and choose the correct answers.

	A	B	C	
(1)	hěn dà 很大	hěn xīn 很新	hěn duō 很多	(　)
(2)	dì-sì gè 第四个	zuì dà de 最大的	zuì xiǎo de 最小的	(　)
(3)	fànguǎn 饭馆	shāngdiàn 商店	xuéxiào 学校	(　)
(4)	wǔ fēnzhōng 五分钟	shí fēnzhōng 十分钟	èrshí fēnzhōng 二十分钟	(　)
(5)	yí gè 一个	liǎng gè 两个	sān gè 三个	(　)

口语练习 Speaking Drills

5 听后重复。 11-8

Listen and repeat.

(1) ______

(2) ______

(3) ______

(4) ______

(5) ______

6 听后回答。 11-9

Listen and answer.

(1) ______

(2) ______

(3) ______

(4) ______

(5) ______

7 回答问题。

Answer the question.

Qǐng jièshào yíxià nǐ de jiā. Jiā zài nǎr? Fángzi shì zěnyàng de? Pángbiān yǒu shénme?
请介绍一下你的家。（家在哪儿？房子是怎样的？旁边有什么？）

______

______

12 Lesson Twelve

Zuótiān wǒmen kǎowánshì le
昨天我们考完试了

We finished our exams yesterday

热身 Warm-up

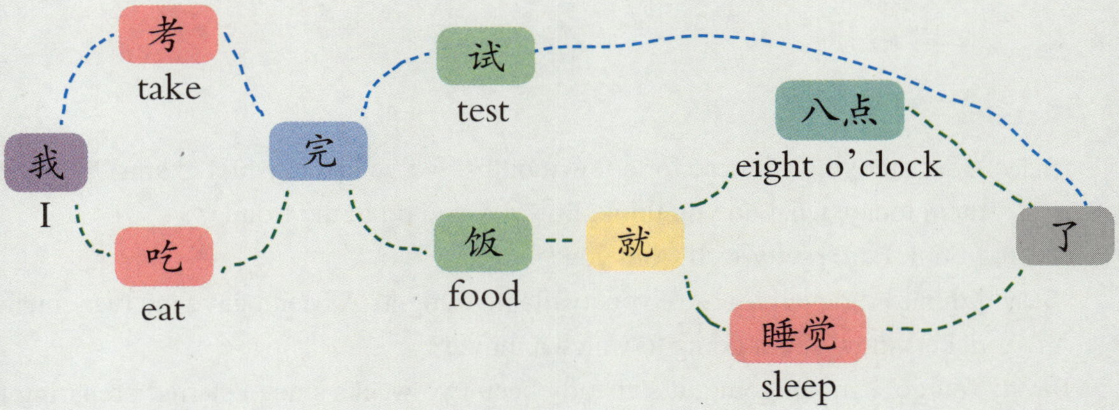

课文 Text

课文 1 12-1

Shālì: Xuéle jǐ gè yuè Zhōngwén, zhè shì dì-yī cì kǎoshì, jīntiān kǎowán shì le, nǐ juéde kǎo de zěnmeyàng?
莎莉：学了几个月中文，这是第一次考试，今天考完试了，你觉得考得怎么样？

Dàwèi: Wǒ juéde kǎo de hái kěyǐ. Nǐ ne?
大卫：我觉得考得还可以。你呢？

Shālì: Wǒ yě juéde hái kěyǐ. Wǎnshang yǒu shíjiān ma? Péngyou gěile wǒ liǎng zhāng diànyǐng piào, wǒmen wǎnshang qù kàn diànyǐng zěnmeyàng?
莎莉：我也觉得还可以。晚上有时间吗？朋友给了我两张电影票，我们晚上去看电影怎么样？

Dàwèi: Nǐ qù ba, wǒ bú qù le, cóng kāishǐ zhǔnbèi kǎoshì dào xiànzài, yǐjīng liǎng gè xīngqī le, xiànzài kǎowán shì le, wǒ yào hǎohǎo shuì jǐ tiān. Xièxie nǐ.
大卫：你去吧，我不去了，从开始准备考试到现在，已经两个星期了，现在考完试了，我要好好睡几天。谢谢你。

Text One

Sally: After studying Chinese for a few months, we've had our first exams. We finished them today, what do you think, how did you do in the exams?

David: I think I did pretty well. And you?

Sally: I think I did well too. Are you available tonight? A friend gave me two cinema tickets, how about going to watch a movie?

David: You go, I'm not going, it's already been two weeks since I started preparing for the exams, now that they're done, I want to sleep well for a few days. Thank you.

课文 2 12-2

Shālì: Zuótiān nǐ xiūxi de zěnmeyàng?
莎莉：昨天你休息得怎么样？

Dàwèi: Wǒ shuì de hěn hǎo. Cóng zuótiān wǎnshang jiǔ diǎn dào jīntiān shàngwǔ jiǔ diǎn,
大卫：我睡得很好。从昨天晚上九点到今天上午九点，

wǒ shuìle shí'èr gè xiǎoshí . Zuótiān
我睡了十二个小时。昨天

de diànyǐng hǎo kàn ma ?
的电影好看吗？

Shālì : Wǒ méi qù kàn diànyǐng .
莎莉：我没去看电影。

Dàwèi : Nǐ zěnme méi qù ne ?
大卫：你怎么没去呢？

Shālì : Zuótiān wǎnshang wǒ chīwán fàn jiù bā diǎn le , diànyǐng qī diǎn jiù kāishǐ le .
莎莉：昨天晚上我吃完饭就八点了，电影七点就开始了。

Text Two

Sally: How was your rest yesterday?

David: I slept very well. Starting at nine o'clock last night until nine o'clock this morning, I slept for 12 hours. Was it a good movie yesterday?

Sally: I didn't go to the cinema.

David: How come you didn't go?

Sally: It was past eight when I finished eating last night, the movie started at seven.

课文3 12–3

Zuótiān wǒmen kǎowánshì le . Shālì xiǎng
昨天我们考完试了。莎莉想

wǎnshang qù kàn diànyǐng , dànshì yīnwèi wǒ juéde
晚上去看电影，但是因为我觉得

hěn lèi , suǒyǐ wǒ xiǎng zài jiā shuìjiào , bù xiǎng qù
很累，所以我想在家睡觉，不想去

kàn diànyǐng le . Wǒ cóng wǎnshang jiǔ diǎn kāishǐ shuìjiào , shuìle shí'èr gè xiǎoshí .
看电影了。我从晚上九点开始睡觉，睡了十二个小时。

Míngtiān jiù yào huí guó le , jīntiān xiàwǔ wǒ zài qù gěi jiārén mǎi diǎnr dōngxi .
明天就要回国了，今天下午我再去给家人买点儿东西。

Text Three

We finished our exams yesterday. Sally wanted to go watch a movie in the evening, but because I was feeling very tired, I wanted to sleep at home, didn't want to go watch a movie. I started sleeping at nine o'clock, and slept for 12 hours. I'm going back to my home country tomorrow, so I'll go buy some more stuff for my family this afternoon.

生词 New Words

考	kǎo	v.	to take a test or exam
有时间	yǒu shíjiān		to be available, to have time
张	zhāng	m.	*used with paper or tickets*
票	piào	n.	ticket
好看	hǎokàn	adj.	good-looking, pretty, nice
回国	huí guó		to go back to one's country / motherland
家人	jiārén	n.	family (member)
点儿	diǎnr	num.	a little

语法点 Language Points

1 结果补语"完"：可以做动词的结果补语，表示结束的意思。例如：

The complement of result "完": it acts as the verb's complement of result and indicates that something has ended. For example:

今天我们考完试了。

We finished our exams today.

做完运动后，你累不累？

Do you feel tired after exercising?

你吃完饭了吗？

Have you finished eating?

2 "还可以"：表示对事物比较满意的态度或评价。例如：

"还可以": it expresses a relatively satisfied attitude or appraisal towards something. For example:

A: 这件衣服怎么样？

A: What do you think about this garment?

B:（这件衣服）还可以。

B: (This garment) is okay.

A: 今天累不累？

A: Are you tired today?

B: 还可以。

B: Not too bad.

我觉得他唱歌唱得还可以。

I think he sings pretty well.

3 形容词重叠“好好”：有些单音节形容词按AA式重叠后可以在句中作状语，表示程度深。例如：

The reduplicated adjective “好好”: some monosyllabic adjectives may be reduplicated according to the AA pattern and form the adverbial adjunct, used to indicate a high degree. For example:

你要好好学习。

You have to study hard.

你要好好吃饭。

You have to eat properly.

你要多多运动。

You have to exercise often.

4 副词“就”：用在时间词语前，表示说话人认为时间晚。例如：

The adverb “就”: when used before a word that expresses time, it indicates that the speaker believes the time of the action is late. For example:

我吃完饭就八点了。

It was (already) eight o'clock when I finished eating.

我回到家就十点了。

It was (already) ten o'clock when I got back home.

我们学完这本书就十二月了。

It'll be December by the time we finish studying this book.

5 “就要……了”：“就”和“要”连用，表示动作行为将要发生，时间比较紧迫，句尾常用语气助词“了”。例如：

“就要……了”: “就” and “要” are used together to indicate that an action or behavior is about to happen and that time is pressing. They are commonly used together with the modal particle “了” placed at the end of the sentence. For example:

我明天就要回国了。

I'm going back to my home country (right) tomorrow.

下星期就要考试了。

Our exams are (just) next week.

出租车就要到了。

The taxi is about to arrive.

练习 Drills

听力练习 Listening Drills

1 听词语，判断图片是否正确。 12-4

Listen to the words and determine whether the pictures are correct.

(1) ______

(2) ______

(3) ______

(4) ______

(5) ______

2 听句子，选择正确图片。 12-5

Listen to the sentences and choose the correct pictures.

(1)

A

B

C

(2)

A

B

C

(3)

A

B

C

（4）

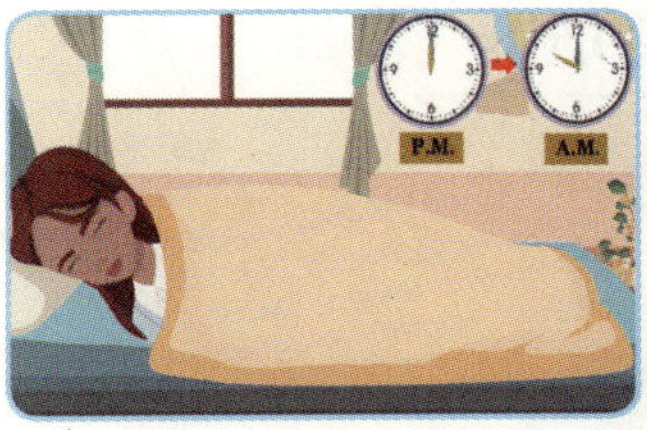

A

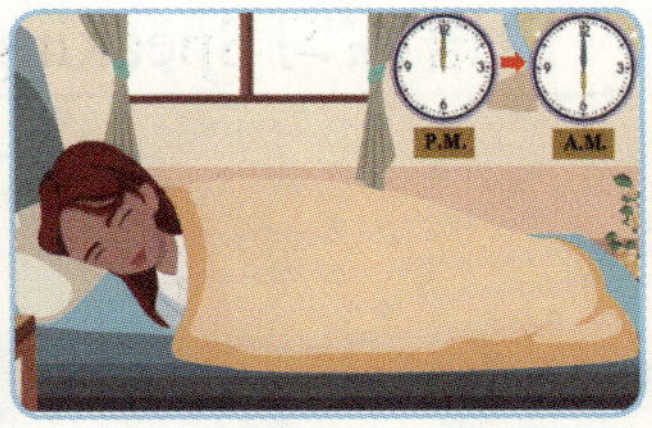

B

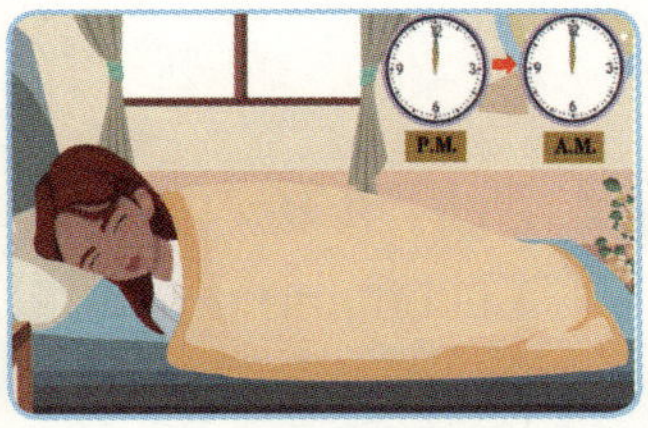

C

（5）

A

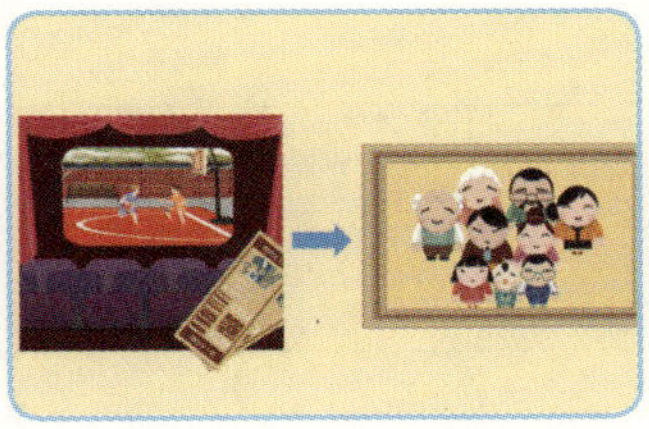
B

C

3 听对话，选择正确图片。 12–6
Listen to the conversations and choose the correct pictures.

A

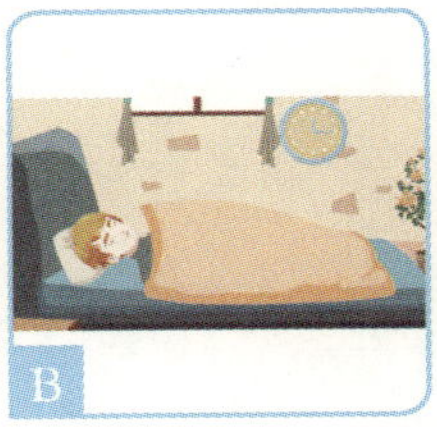
B

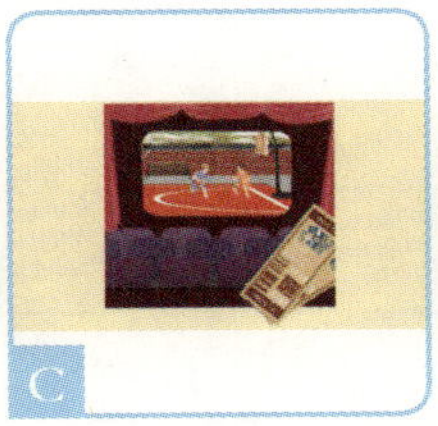
C

D

E

（1）		（2）	
（3）		（4）	
（5）			

4 听录音，选择正确答案。 12–7
Listen to the recordings and choose the correct answers.

（1）	A. dì-yī cì 第一次	B. dì-èr cì 第二次	C. hěn duō cì 很多次	（ ）
（2）	A. bù hǎo 不好	B. bù zhīdào 不知道	C. hái kěyǐ 还可以	（ ）
（3）	A. qián 钱	B. diànyǐngpiào 电影票	C. yào 药	（ ）
（4）	A. liǎng gè xīngqī 两个星期	B. yí gè xīngqī 一个星期	C. liǎng gè yuè 两个月	（ ）
（5）	A. mǎi piào 买票	B. mǎi dōngxi 买东西	C. mǎi yīfu 买衣服	（ ）

口语练习 Speaking Drills

5 听后重复。 11-8
Listen and repeat.

(1) ______
(2) ______
(3) ______
(4) ______
(5) ______

6 听后回答。 11-9
Listen and answer.

(1) ______
(2) ______
(3) ______
(4) ______
(5) ______

7 选词填空，读一读。
Fill in the blanks with the words and then read the text.

A. 完 wán　B. 要 yào　C. 从 cóng　D. 想 xiǎng　E. 再 zài

Zuótiān wǒmen kǎo（　）shì le, Shālì（　）wǎnshang qù kàn diànyǐng. Yīnwèi wǒ juéde hěn lèi, suǒyǐ wǒ xiǎng zài jiā shuìjiào, bù xiǎng qù kàn diànyǐng le. Wǒ（　）wǎnshang jiǔ diǎn kāishǐ shuìjiào, shuìle shí'èr gè xiǎoshí. Míngtiān jiù（　）huí guó le, jīntiān xiàwǔ wǒ（　）qù gěi jiārén mǎi diǎnr dōngxi.

昨天我们考（　）试了，莎莉（　）晚上去看电影。因为我觉得很累，所以我想在家睡觉，不想去看电影了。我（　）晚上九点开始睡觉，睡了十二个小时。明天就（　）回国了，今天下午我（　）去给家人买点儿东西。

词汇总表 Vocabulary

生词 New Words

词语 Word / Phrase	拼音 *Pinyin*	词性 Part of Speech	词义 Meaning	课号 Lesson
		B		
吧	bā	part.	*indicates a suggestion*	1
百	bǎi	num.	hundred	6
半	bàn	num.	half	3
帮助	bāngzhù	v. / n.	to help; help	7
报纸	bàozhǐ	n.	newspaper	5
本	běn	m.	*use with books*	1
比	bǐ	prep.	than	6
别	bié	adv.	do not	5
不要	bú yào	adv.	do not	5
		C		
长	cháng	adj.	long	6
车钱	chē qián		fare	6
出（来）	chū (lái)	v.	to come out, to get out	3
出租车	chūzūchē	n.	taxi	6
穿	chuān	v.	(of clothes) to wear,to put on	3
次	cì	m.	*indicates the number of times sth. is done or experienced*	3
从	cóng	prep.	from	4
错	cuò	adj.	wrong, incorrect	2
		D		
打（篮球）	dǎ (lánqiú)	v.	to play (basketball)	4
大家	dàjiā	pron.	everybody, everyone	5
但是	dànshì	conj.	but, however	4
到	dào	v.	to arrive, to get to, to reach	4
得	dé	part.	*indicates the result or degree*	4

续表

词语 Word / Phrase	拼音 *Pinyin*	词性 Part of Speech	词义 Meaning	课号 Lesson
等	děng	v.	to wait	3
地铁	dìtiě	n.	subway	6
第二	dì-èr	num.	second	3
第一	dì-yī	num.	first	3
点儿	diǎnr	num.	a little	12
电话号码	diànhuà hàomǎ		telephone number	9
对	duì	prep.	to, for	5
对	duì	adj.	right, correct	2
		F		
房间	fángjiān	n.	room	7
房子	fángzi	n.	house	11
非常	fēicháng	adv.	very, extremely	3
服务员	fúwùyuán	n.	attendant, waiter / waitress	9
		G		
高	gāo	adj.	tall	7
告诉	gàosu	v.	to tell	3
给	gěi	v. / prep.	give, (*used after a verb*) to, for	1
公共汽车	gōnggòng qìchē	n.	bus	6
贵	guì	adj.	expensive	6
过	guo	part.	*used after a verb to indicate a past action or state*	8
		H		
还	hái	adv.	still, in addtion	3
还没	hái méi		not yet	7
好看	hǎo kàn	adj.	good-looking, pretty, nice	12
红	hóng	adj.	red	2
红色	hóngsè	n.	red	9
后	hòu	n.	after	9
欢迎	huānyíng	v.	to welcome	1
回答	huídá	v.	to answer	11

续表

词语 Word / Phrase	拼音 *Pinyin*	词性 Part of Speech	词义 Meaning	课号 Lesson
回国	huí guó		to go back to one's country / motherland	12
			J	
机场	jīchǎng	n.	airport	6
鸡蛋面	jīdàn miàn		egg noodles	8
家	jiā	m.	*used with companies, restaurants, shops, etc.*	8
家人	jiārén	n.	family (member)	12
见到	jiàndào		to see	10
件	jiàn	m.	*used with items of clothing*	7
叫车	jiàochē		to call for a taxi / car	6
进	jìn	v.	to go in	10
近	jìn	adj.	close	10
觉得	juéde	v.	to feel, to think	2
			K	
咖啡	kāfēi	n.	coffee	1
开	kāi	v.	to turn on	11
开始	kāishǐ	v.	to begin, to start	4
开（药）	kāi (yào)	v.	to prescribe medicine	10
看（到）	kàn (dào)	v.	to see	9
考	kǎo	v.	to take a test or exam	12
考试	kǎoshì	n.	test, exam	11
可能	kěnéng	aux.	maybe, probably	2
客气	kèqi	adj.	polite	1
可以	kěyǐ	aux. / adj.	can, may; to be able to	6
快	kuài	adj.	fast, quick	3
快乐	kuàilè	adj.	happy	10
			L	
篮球	lánqiú	n.	basketball	4
老	lǎo	adj.	old	6
累	lèi	adj.	tired	5
离	lí	v.	to be away from, to be at a distance from	10

续表

词语 Word / Phrase	拼音 *Pinyin*	词性 Part of Speech	词义 Meaning	课号 Lesson
路	lù	n.	road	11
			M	
慢	màn	adj.	slow	11
每	měi	pron.	every	4
门	mén	n.	door	3
			N	
那天	nà tiān		that day	10
			P	
旁边	pángbiān	n.	beside	11
跑	pǎo	v.	to run	4
跑步	pǎobù	v. / n.	to run; running	4
便宜	piányi	adj.	cheap	6
票	piào	n.	ticket	12
			Q	
妻子	qīzi	n.	wife	10
起床	qǐchuáng	v.	to get out of bed, to get up	3
前	qián	n.	front, in front	10
晴	qíng	adj.	sunny	2
			R	
让	ràng	v.	to let	9
			S	
上课	shàngkè	v.	to have a class	2
身体	shēntǐ	n.	body	5
生日	shēngrì	n.	birthday	10
时间	shíjiān	n.	time	6
手机	shǒujī	n.	cellphone	5
书	shū	n.	book	1
睡	shuì	v.	to sleep, to nap	5
虽然	suīrán	conj.	although	11
所以	suǒyǐ	conj.	so, therefore	10
			T	
它	tā	pron.	it	5

续表

词语 Word / Phrase	拼音 *Pinyin*	词性 Part of Speech	词义 Meaning	课号 Lesson
踢（足球）	tī (zúqiú)	v.	to play (soccer)	4
听说	tīngshuō	v.	to hear, to learn about, to be told	6
			W	
外（面）	wài (miàn)	n.	outside	11
完	wán	v.	to finish	11
玩	wán	v.	to play	3
晚上	wǎnshang	n.	evening, night	2
问	wèn	v.	to ask	1
问题	wèntí	n.	question	11
午觉	wǔjiào	n.	noontime nap	5
			X	
下面	xiàmiàn	n.	under	9
小时	xiǎoshí	n.	hour	3
新	xīn	adj.	new	6
休息	xiūxi	v.	to have a rest	7
学会	xuéhuì	v.	to learn, to master	8
雪	xuě	n.	snow	2
雪人	xuěrén	n.	snowman	3
			Y	
眼睛	yǎnjing	n.	eye	2
羊肉	yángròu	n.	mutton	1
要	yào	aux.	to be about / going to	2
要	yào	aux.	should, have to	6
也	yě	adv.	also, too	2
一点儿	yìdiǎnr	num.	a bit, a little, some	7
一会儿	yíhuìr	num.	a little while	5
一起	yìqǐ	adv.	together	1
已经	yǐjīng	adv.	already	3
因为	yīnwèi	conj.	because, as	2
阴	yīn	adj.	overcast, cloudy	2
用	yòng	v.	to use	11
游泳	yóuyǒng	v.	to swim	4

续表

词语 Word / Phrase	拼音 *Pinyin*	词性 Part of Speech	词义 Meaning	课号 Lesson
有点儿	yǒudiǎnr	adv.	a little	2
有时候	yǒu shíhou		sometimes	5
有时间	yǒu shíjiān		to be available, to have time	12
有事儿	yǒushìr		to have sth. on one's mind; to be preoccupied (*here used to asked what the matter is*)	9
右边	yòubian	n.	right side	11
鱼	yú	n.	fish	1
远	yuǎn	adj.	far	6
运动	yùndòng	n. / v.	sports; to exercise	4
		Z		
再	zài	adv.	again, once more	3
早上	zǎoshang	n.	morning	2
张	zhāng	m.	*used with paper or tickets*	12
找	zhǎo	v.	to look for, to try to find	9
着	zhe	part.	*used after a verb or an adjective to indicate the continuation of an action or a state*	11
真	zhēn	adv.	really, indeed	4
真的	zhēn de	adv.	really	3
正在	zhèngzài	adv.	right now, in the process / course of	3
知道	zhīdào	v.	to know	2
祝	zhù	v.	to wish	10
准备	zhǔnbèi	v.	to prepare	11
走	zǒu	v.	to leave, to walk	2
走路	zǒulù	v.	to walk	10
租	zū	v.	to rent	10
足球	zúqiú	n.	soccer, football	4
最	zuì	adv.	most, to the greatest extent	1
左边	zuǒbian	n.	left side	11
做（菜）	zuò (cài)	v.	to cook	8